▶ **Global Politics of Health Reform in Africa**

DOI: 10.1057/9781137500151.0001

Other Palgrave Pivot titles

DOI: 10.1057/9781137500151.0001

palgrave▸**pivot**

Global Politics of Health Reform in Africa: Performance, Participation, and Policy

Amy Barnes

Lecturer in International Health Policy and Management, University of Sheffield, UK

Garrett Wallace Brown

Reader in Political Theory and Global Ethics, University of Sheffield, UK

and

Sophie Harman

Reader in International Politics, Queen Mary University of London, UK

palgrave
macmillan

DOI: 10.1057/9781137500151.0001

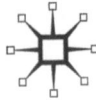
First published 2015 by
PALGRAVE MACMILLAN

Palgrave Macmillan in the UK is an imprint of Macmillan Publishers Limited, registered in England, company number 785998, of Houndmills, Basingstoke, Hampshire RG21 6XS.

Palgrave Macmillan in the US is a division of St Martin's Press LLC, 175 Fifth Avenue, New York, NY 10010.

Palgrave Macmillan is the global academic imprint of the above companies and has companies and representatives throughout the world.

Palgrave® and Macmillan® are registered trademarks in the United States, the United Kingdom, Europe and other countries.

ISBN: 978–1–137–50016–8 EPub
ISBN: 978–1–137–50015–1 PDF
ISBN: 978–1–137–50014–4 Hardback

A catalogue record for this book is available from the British Library.

A catalog record for this book is available from the Library of Congress.

www.palgrave.com/pivot

DOI: 10.1057/9781137500151

Contents

List of Illustrations

Figures

▶

Tables

DOI: 10.1057/9781137500151.0002

Acknowledgements

The research underpinning this book is drawn from a wider research programme led by the Regional Network for Equity in Health in East and Southern Africa (EQUINET, www.equinetafrica.org) through Training and Research Support Centre (TARSC) and the University of Carleton focusing on the participation of African actors in global health diplomacy, funded by the International Development Research Centre (Canada) and carried out in cooperation with the East Southern and Central Africa (ECSA) Health Community. Through case studies, of which the work in this book is a part, the programme, working with government officials in health and diplomacy, with technical institutions, civil society, and other stakeholders in east and southern African countries, examines the role of global health diplomacy (GHD), including south–south diplomacy, in addressing selected key challenges to health and strengthening health systems, and is using the evidence and learning to inform African policy actors and stakeholders within processes of health diplomacy. Sections of this book have previously been published in Barnes et al. (2014) 'African participation and partnership in performance based funding: a case study in global health policy' published by the Regional Network on Equity in Health in Southern Africa (EQUINET) Discussion Paper 102, EQUINET, Harare (http://www.equinetafrica.org/bibl/docs/GHD%20Gov%20Diss%20Paper%20102.pdf) and are used with permission of EQUINET. The authors would like to acknowledge and thank Patrick Banda, Robyn Hayes, and Chishimba

Mulambia, Ministry of Health, Zambia, South Africa, Institute of Social and Economic Research, University of Zambia, as research team members in the EQUINET work and the peer reviewers, colleagues in EQUINET, and others who supported and gave review input to the work. The authors acknowledge that they alone are responsible for the views expressed in the use of this work in this publication and that they do not necessarily represent the official views, decisions, or policies of the EQUINET steering committee or any of the partner institutions acknowledged.

The authors are grateful to all the research participants who agreed to be interviewed, recommended reports to read, arranged participant observation of meetings, and generally obliged the research process. The authors would also like to give a wholehearted thanks to Andreas Papamichail for his work on the earlier discussion paper as well as his general support throughout the research project.

Ethical approval was secured from the University of Sheffield Research Ethics Committee (REC), the University of Zambia REC, the Ministry of Health Zambia, Tanzania Commission for Science and Technology (COSTECH), and the Human Sciences Research Council South Africa.

Sophie Harman would like to thank Natalie Wright for supporting her research through the provision of free accommodation and friends in Zambia; Kieran Read and Zephania Maduhu for their support in Tanzania; Hank and Lucy Arrington for their warm hospitality in Washington, DC; and the School of Politics and International Relations at Queen Mary for the research leave to do the fieldwork. Garrett Brown would like to thank the Department of Health Western Cape, South Africa, for hosting one of the workshops associated with this research; John Vance for the free accommodation while conducting research in Cape Town; Gemma Bennett for her quick grant accounting and field-work support; Rene Loewenson for her intellectual contributions; and Mihaela Gruia for her research assistance during the literature review phase.

List of Abbreviations

ANC	Antenatal Care
AZT	Azidothymidine
CBoH	Central Board of Health (Zambia)
CCM	Country Co-ordinating Mechanism
CDC	Centers for Disease Control and Prevention
CHAI	Clinton Health Access Initiative
CHAZ	Churches Health Association of Zambia
CSSC	Christian Social Services Commission (Tanzania)
DfID	Department for International Development
ECSA HC	East, Central and Southern African Health Community
HMIS	Health Management Information System
HRITF	Health Results Innovation Trust Fund
ITN	Insecticide-Treated Nets
LFA	Local Fund Agent
MCHCD	Ministry of Mother Child Health and Community Development
MDG	Millennium Development Goal
MNCH	Maternal Newborn Child Health
MoH	Ministry of Health (Zambia)
MoHSW	Ministry of Health and Social Welfare (Tanzania)
NAC	National HIV/AIDS/STI/TB Council (Zambia)
NHS	National Health Service (South Africa)
NORAD	Norwegian Agency for Development Cooperation
NSP	National Strategic Plan (South Africa)

DOI: 10.1057/9781137500151.0004

P4P	Pay-for-Performance
PBF	Performance-Based Funding
PEPFAR	President's Emergency Plan for AIDS Relief
PR	Principal Recipient
PWC	PriceWaterhouseCoopers
RBF	Results-Based Funding
SADC	Southern Africa Development Committee
SANAC	South African National AIDS Council
SR	Sub-recipient
SWAps	Sector-Wide Approaches
TACAIDS	Tanzania Commission for AIDS
TNCM	Tanzania National Coordinating Mechanism
TRP	Technical Review Panel (Global Fund)
UNAIDS	Joint United Nations Programme on HIV/AIDS
UNDP	United Nations Development Programme
UNFPA	United Nations Population Fund
USAID	United States Agency for International Development
WHO	World Health Organization

DOI: 10.1057/9781137500151.0004

1

Introduction: Global Politics of Health Reform in Africa

Abstract: *Participation and performance have become two master concepts for wider health reform in Africa. These concepts were initially used in the delivery of HIV/AIDS and maternal and newborn child health programmes as part of the UN Millennium Development Goals; however, key international donors such as the World Bank and the Global Fund to Fight AIDS, Tuberculosis and Malaria are now seeing the potential of such concepts in mechanisms of wider health reform in Africa. This chapter introduces the context, aims, and argument of the book and provides a detailed account of the qualitative methods used to conduct research in South Africa, Tanzania, and Zambia and two global health hubs: Geneva and Washington, DC.*

Keywords: Global Fund; health reform; HIV/AIDS; maternal and newborn child health (MNCH); qualitative research; World Bank

Barnes Amy, Garrett Wallace Brown and Sophie Harman. *Global Politics of Health Reform in Africa: Performance, Participation, and Policy.* Basingstoke: Palgrave Macmillan, 2015. DOI: 10.1057/9781137500151.0005.

The health of the population of sub-Saharan Africa has long been a pre-occupation of global health actors, policies, and spending. Over the last 20 years this pre-occupation has led to a surge in intergovernmental organisations, non-governmental organisations, and public–private partnerships and reconfigurations of government agencies in an attempt to throw money and research at a myriad of African health problems, from extensively drug-resistant tuberculosis (XDR-TB) to diarrheal diseases. Interest in and commitment to the health of Africans in many respects reached its zenith with the inclusion of three health-related goals – combat HIV/AIDS, malaria, and tuberculosis; maternal mortality; child mortality – in the United Nations 2000 Millennium Development Goals (MDGs). The MDGs opened the floodgates for new interventions and actors in response to the three health goals and presented a call to arms for the international community to combat HIV/AIDS in particular. In the period immediately following the MDGs for example, development assistance for HIV/AIDS rose rapidly from $0.8 billion in 2000 to $5.1 billion in 2007 (Ravishankar et al., 2009). Yet, despite significant progress in some areas such as HIV awareness and access to anti-retroviral therapy, and growing attention to issues such as maternal health, progress towards improving the physical and mental health of the population of Africa has been slow (African Union Commission et al., 2013; WHO, 2014a). The World Health Statistics 2014 show, for example, that the risk of a child dying before their fifth birthday remains highest in Africa (95 per 1,000 live births) and that people living in sub-Saharan Africa account for an estimated 70% of those newly infected with HIV (WHO, 2014a). Increasingly global health actors have come to realise that a major stumbling block to the realisation of better health for all Africans is the tricky issue of health system reform.

Health system reform in Africa is a difficult subject because of questions about who is responsible for the articulation of what reforms should exist (an elected government or the myriad of international donors and external agencies that fund the health system), what kind of reform is desired, who will pay for reform, and how reform should be implemented. Moreover to speak of health reform requires a greater engagement with health systems, a concept so broad it can apply to hospitals and medical centres, clinicians and their training, research and salaries, procurement and logistics, and mechanisms of health system financing. It has also created a whole body of research as to what the most effective and equitable health system would look like (see, e.g., Frenk, 2009; 2010;

DOI: 10.1057/9781137500151.0005

Sheikh et al., 2011). Actors within the global health community such as the World Bank entered these debates and initiated projects in the 1980s and early 1990s and were not thanked for their efforts. They were criticised, for example, for not fully engaging with the local populations for which the reforms were meant to serve, undermining the sovereignty of the state, under-funding health systems through cuts to public spending, and prioritising the private sector (Laurell and Arellano, 1996; Harman, 2009). Other global health actors such as the Bill and Melinda Gates Foundation have steered clear of health system reform altogether, cognisant of the politics of such efforts and the inability to make a measurable impact in this as a distinct area of reform. Health system reform since 2000 thus came to be a covert strategy: an issue that was not discussed or included as part of wider health strategies in Africa under the MDGs, but something that would occur in and through a multitude of vertical interventions such as national malaria plans and neglected tropical disease strategies.

Health system reform in Africa is, however, now back as a specific item on the agenda in global health politics. It is back on the agenda in a way that attempts to overcome the problems of state ownership and sovereignty, competing donor strategies, and how to measure success and impact, while managing health system reform in the wider context of the MDGs. The current framing of health system reform in Africa is the consequence of three trends in global health policy. The first is the need for measurement and performance as articulated by the MDGs and adopted as the norm of health development financing by Western donors. The second trend is the emphasis on collaboration and state-led initiatives rather than top-down donor-led projects. This was encapsulated by the World Bank's Poverty Reduction Strategy Papers and Comprehensive Development Framework approach to working with African governments and the Paris Declaration on aid effectiveness that stressed ownership, results, and accountability. The third trend has been the changing position of what were 'the big three' diseases under the MDGs: HIV/AIDS, malaria, and tuberculosis. Efforts to combat these three diseases now need to stress the benefits for wider health systems and health reform more broadly, in order to justify continued investment and maintain relevance as debates in global health policy shift. Combined these three trends have generated two master concepts for health reform in Africa: participation and performance.

DOI: 10.1057/9781137500151.0005

Participation is a key policy concept in global health, and has a long and varied genealogy in global development thinking and practice (Hickey and Mohan, 2004). In its most basic understanding, participation in global health relates to the ability of stakeholders to engage with and shape health policy at four intersecting levels: local, national, regional, and global. Such engagement continues to remain the main normative aim behind debates about furthering more equitable health diplomacy and, as a result, has been increasingly integrated into the agenda of global agencies. Participation has been integrated as a guiding concept in the World Health Organization's (WHO) latest Programme of Work 2014–2019 (WHO, 2014a: 19). It is a guiding principle of the Global Fund to Fight AIDS, Tuberculosis and Malaria (hereafter the Global Fund, 2001), which rose to prominence on the back of the advocacy campaigns about universal access to anti-retroviral therapy to treat HIV/AIDS, and also an operational principle of the World Bank (2014). Participation is also the master concept underwriting the MDGs, specifically Goal 8: 'To develop a partnership for development.' Within policy statements and discussions, participation is often seen as having a normative value (something we ought to strengthen for moral reasons) as well as having practical relevance (a governance mechanism that will produce more equitable and effective outcomes for health). Yet, the role of participation in establishing more robust global health partnerships remains under-theorised and under-examined (Barnes and Brown, 2011), particularly in relation to how local and governmental actors can or should participate as effective participants in (1) the formulation of African health reform; (2) the conception and design of related health system interventions; and (3) their subsequent implementation.

In relation to performance, the greatest application of the idea in health system reform has been through results or performance-based funding, or PBF, specifically relating to the areas of maternal and newborn child health (MNCH), and HIV/AIDS, malaria, and tuberculosis programmes. PBF refers to the idea of transferring resources (money, material goods) on condition that particular actions are taken or specific, predefined performance targets are achieved (Eldridge and Palmer, 2009). The conditional transfer of money or material goods is believed to be key to PBF, as it provides the incentive for performance within health systems. It is because of this that PBF is increasingly promoted by leading global actors as a way to efficiently and effectively reform the way that health systems are planned, financed, co-ordinated, and steered, particularly in low- and middle-income countries. Key international donors such as the Global Fund and World Bank argue that PBF will promote reform in a way that is locally owned and accountable (Witter et al., 2012), given that performance targets will be developed or negotiated through active participation of local actors from the bottom-up, rather than being set by global agencies from the top-down. While the term PBF is used within the context of this research, it is important to highlight that a range of different terms are used to signify this type of health system intervention. These include:

- performance-based funding
- performance-based financing
- performance-based contracting
- pay for performance
- results-based funding
- results-based financing
- output-based aid
- value for money
- buy-downs

PBF can apply to both supply-side and demand-side means of facilitating results and performance. Supply-side PBF programmes tend to involve giving health workers or health centres financial incentives to encourage the provision of services. For example, financial rewards might be offered if a specific number of women deliver their baby in a health clinic per month. Demand-side PBF programmes focus on the users of health services and tend to involve providing monetary incentives to attend and use services that are on offer. For example, 'mama kits' are offered as a way to incentivise pregnant women to deliver in health centres or hospitals. This book is principally interested in supply-side PBF programmes; however, PBF schemes will often involve elements of both. While there are variations in the way that PBF schemes are conceived, designed, and implemented, common to all is the idea that positive health system reforms can be incentivised and brought about by tying the transfer of resources to predefined performance targets.

It is these two concepts – participation and performance – that are the concern of this book. Participation and PBF have been increasingly used as models for HIV/AIDS and MNCH by international donors such as the World Bank, United States Agency for International Development (USAID), Cordaid, the Clinton Health Access Initiative (CHAI) of the

DOI: 10.1057/9781137500151.0005

William J Clinton Foundation, the Norwegian Agency for Development Cooperation (NORAD), and the Global Fund. However, there is now growing rhetoric from donors such as the USAID and countries such as Rwanda that such initiatives could hold the key to wider success in health system reform in Africa. The purpose of this book is to critically reflect on how participation and PBF have been applied to the management of health systems and what such application tells us about the future of health reform in Africa. The aim of the book is to investigate how and why PBF and participation have come to prominence as an ideational policy concept, to trace the history of PBF as a tool of health policy reform, to see how participation works at multiple levels of health governance, and crucially to identify the extent to which African actors shape health reform in African countries. It provides a critical examination of the application of these two concepts to health reform in South Africa, Tanzania, and Zambia. In so doing, the book investigates how different actors understand participation and performance, the evidence behind the policy rhetoric about PBF success, and the wider politics associated with how actors participate and measure performance. Existing debate in global health and development policy has shown a favourable bias to performance and participation by focusing on the positive externalities of these two concepts with little engagement with the agency of different people (including government ministries, health facilities, civil society) in these African countries. This book addresses this lacuna. It is about the politics of how participation and performance are used to shape health reform in Africa and the role of African actors in reforming health systems in African countries.

Analytical framework

The book takes a multi-level governance approach to exploring the use of participation and performance as tools of health reform in Africa. Multi-level governance refers to the sharing of authority and policy-making across sub-national, national, and supranational levels of government (Marks et al., 1996), as well as the public, private, and voluntary sector (Bache and Chapman, 2008). The state is still of paramount concern and multi-level governance has a statist core, but it is assumed that it does not have monopoly over decision-making and instead must share power (Eising, 2004). More specifically, it is assumed that sub-national

DOI: 10.1057/9781137500151.0005

decision-making exists beyond the scope or 'nest' of the state (Marks et al., 1996) and that shared sovereignty exists in that external actors (international agencies and donors) have influence over domestic authority (Mamudu and Studlar, 2009).

The use of a multi-level analysis allows for a conceptualisation of global health governance that does not isolate or ignore the state in the same way that regime-based or transnational understandings are said to do (Betsill and Bulkeley, 2006). At the same time, multi-level governance provides space for the inclusion of civil society both within and outside processes of global governance as an arena or 'a space for critical reflection and affective expression' (Brassett and Smith, 2010: 414). Different forms of multi-level governance, such as multi sectoral governance that points to the inclusion of all aspects of society in decision-making, shift the focus away from a state-centred, institutional narrative of power and agenda-setting to allow for greater recognition of both deliberations within civil society and between civil society and international institutions. Multi-level governance in this respect confers a degree of 'communicative power' through the use of 'minipublics' (Bohman, 2010: 433) and 'deliberative systems' (Parkinson and Mansbridge, 2013). In this sense, it gives conceptual space to understand the complexity of contemporary forms of governance. This book uses such conceptual space by drawing on a methodology that looks at participation and PBF policy formation at the global, regional, and national level. The book does not take these categories as distinct or locate specific actors within certain levels, but sees multi-level governance in global health policy as fluid and overlapping. This multi-level approach is evident in Figure 1.1, which seeks to visualise the conceptual relationship between participation and PBF and to demonstrate the key questions embedded in this book.

Figure 1.1 illustrates that this book examines how African actors participate in three levels of PBF policy (design, implementation, and accountability), at what levels (global, regional, and national), in what spaces (formal, informal), and with what affect in terms of quality of participation. The aim is to not only look at how such multi-level governance works in practice, but to reveal the political devices and sources of agency used at every level to enact or subvert the wider reform process. Hence the concept of agency, and more critically African agency, has provided a useful analytical lens for revealing the spaces and forms of participation of African actors within this system of multi-level governance. Here we use Brown and Harman's (2013: 2–3)

DOI: 10.1057/9781137500151.0005

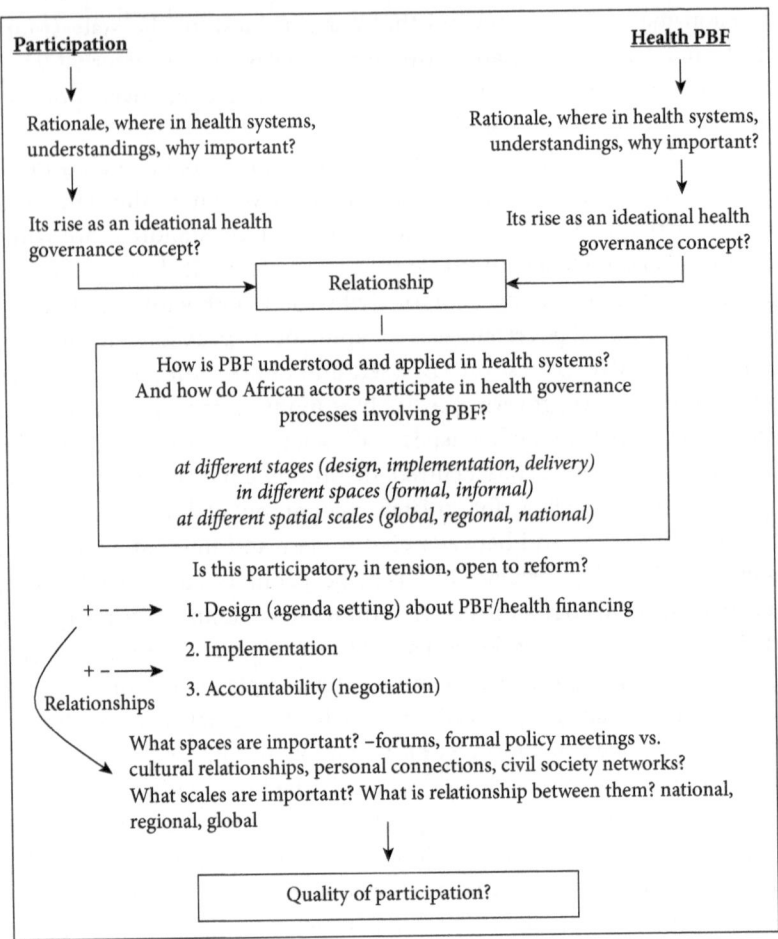

FIGURE 1.1 *The conceptual linkages between participation and performance-based funding (PBF)*

Source: Author construction.

definition of African agency as an intellectual intent to 'get beyond the tired tropes of an Africa that is victimised, chaotic, violent and poor' by asking 'how much influence or power is being exerted and how much freedom of action African political actors have available to them' and what kind of agency is enacted. Agency is used here as a means to assess the extent to which African actors are able to define, influence, shape, reproduce, and resist PBF programmes and participatory processes in African countries.

DOI: 10.1057/9781137500151.0005

Methodology

A multi-level approach to understanding PBF, participation, and the role of African actors in shaping African health reform underpinned the research design. The majority of existing research on PBF rests on quantitative methodologies. This study is different as it is the first of its kind to present extensive and comparative qualitative research in this area. The use of qualitative methodology was a deliberate means of ensuring understanding, from the perspective of African actors themselves, the types of spaces that exist for participation in global health governance relating to PBF. This is because quantitative studies have difficulty in capturing subjective concepts like 'participation' and so a qualitative approach was deemed appropriate here given that the primary aim of the study was to discover how African actors see themselves as meaningful participants within PBF as a mechanism of health system reform. Given the preference for quantitative research in global health policy and by the actors we engage with in this book, the qualitative methods are outlined here in deliberate detail. This is to highlight the depth and rigour of the research in which the book's main findings are based, and to demonstrate the utility of qualitative research in global health policy.

Case studies: South Africa, Tanzania, and Zambia

South Africa, Tanzania, and Zambia were selected as case study countries to give a clear focus for exploring the participation of different African actors in PBF; and comparative insight into the potentially different ways in which such participation can take place. The comparative element comes from the fact that there are similarities and differences in terms of the PBF schemes in operation in each country and in terms of the social, political, and economic context. In terms of similarities at the national level, South Africa, Tanzania, and Zambia all have recent or ongoing PBF projects associated with international donors, and all have been in negotiations with international donors in relation to future scaling up of PBF or extensions to ongoing PBF projects. More specifically, Zambia, Tanzania, and South Africa all have Global Fund projects that are being implemented using PBF, which was deemed an important element for comparison. All Global Fund PBF projects involve disease-specific indicators, outputs, and/or outcomes relating to HIV, malaria, and/or tuberculosis and all are managed through

DOI: 10.1057/9781137500151.0005

similar institutional structures: Country Coordinating Mechanisms, Principal- and Sub-Recipients, and Local Fund Agents. At regional to global levels, all have diplomatic missions in Geneva engaged with the WHO on global health policy and all are members of regional bodies with health policy remits.

In terms of difference, the gross domestic product (GDP) and national reliance on external funding within the health sector (judged by external resources for health as % of total expenditure on health) was significantly different in South Africa, Tanzania, and Zambia. For example, WHO estimates suggest that in 2011 the contribution of external resources for health in Tanzania and Zambia was 40.2% and 27.8%, respectively, and thus was significantly different than in South Africa, which was estimated to have 2.1% reliance on external funding (WHO *World Health Statistics*, 2014). By examining cases with different economic conditions, our research facilitates comparison in terms of how economic (in)dependence might shape participation in the design, implementation, and evaluation of PBF. Each country also had different stated forms of national 'success' in terms of ongoing relationships with international donors about PBF schemes, and particularly in terms of ongoing relationships with the World Bank (who has been key in promoting PBF globally). In Zambia, a PBF pilot project funded by the World Bank (through the Health Results Innovation Trust Fund or HRITF) is at an advanced stage and there is a close relationship between the Ministry of Health and World Bank PBF specialists in the country. In Tanzania, a PBF pilot supported by CHAI is up and running and involves discussions with the World Bank about national scale-up, yet negotiations have stalled more recently. In both countries, the pilots involve paying health professionals when they (or the health facility in which they work) meet certain outputs or outcomes related to service delivery for MNCH. In contrast, there is no PBF scheme involving the World Bank in South Africa – relations were discontinued with the Bank in the past due to disagreements about attached conditionalities, but negotiations have recently reopened in relation to securing support for the roll out of the South African National Health Strategic Plan (NSP-PBF is an element in such discussions). This all suggests differences in the way in which actors within each country engage with and negotiate PBF, and with the World Bank in particular. This is particularly relevant for comparison, given the existence of similar grant/loan conditions that are placed upon each case country by international donors such as the World Bank.

DOI: 10.1057/9781137500151.0005

Given the points made above about similarities and differences in relation to the way PBF associated with the Global Fund and World Bank has been negotiated in each country, the research focused on examining PBF schemes associated with these two global actors in each country (rather than more generally across all PBF schemes). Both the Fund and Bank have high-profile roles in global health governance and have stated their operational commitment to apply PBF approaches within health systems and to work in a participatory way. Focusing on these two organisations was therefore highly relevant in relation to the aims of the study. While both the Global Fund and World Bank are involved in PBF mechanisms, they employ different approaches as outlined in Table 1.1.

It is also important to note that PBF schemes involving the Fund and Bank also tend to involve a range of other actors, including, for example, CHAI, USAID, Cordaid, the UK Department for International Development (DfID), and NORAD. Some of these agencies are partners with the Global Fund and World Bank in facilitating the implementation of PBF in-country. Others such as NORAD have been instrumental in financing and establishing the HRITF of the World Bank that finances and designs PBF programmes. The HRITF is a multi-donor fund created by the World Bank in 2007, with funding from Norway and the UK, to

TABLE 1.1   *Key characteristics of the Global Fund and World Bank's approaches to PBF*

	Types of performance target	Country-based partners
Global Fund	Targets based on disease-specific indicators/outputs/outcomes – HIV/AIDS, malaria, and TB (with health systems strengthening dimensions)	Country Co-ordinating Mechanism (CCM) – multisectoral actors
World Bank	Narrow targets based on payment for service/outcome – increasingly the focus is maternal health (when project/programme based), for example, results-based financing and pay-for-performance Also contributes to targets as part of wider health reform programmes and MDGs (but this is case specific) Maternal and newborn child health (MNCH)	Managed through state/MoH project teams District or facility based and/or may be targeted at individual health professionals Often combined with resources transfers to communities

DOI: 10.1057/9781137500151.0005

support the development of health-related PBF (HRITF, 2014a). Total current commitments to the fund are equivalent to US$537 million and are linked to $2.4 billion in IDA (International Development Association) financing (ibid.). The HRITF not only provides country pilot grants to support the design, implementation, and evaluation of PBF programmes (such as the project underway in Zambia), but also provides financing for knowledge and learning.

In addition to looking at PBF schemes involving the Global Fund and World Bank in South Africa, Tanzania, and Zambia, a decision was made to also examine the WHO as a potentially key interfacing actor within PBF and health reform, because of the global role that the institution maintains regarding health policy uniformity at both global and national levels. Given this, it was necessary to consider whether the WHO had any kind of 'shaping' role in how participation and PBF operate in relation to both the Global Fund and World Bank.

Research methods

To develop a detailed understanding of the historical development of PBF in the arena of global health, a detailed policy and literature review was carried out. This involved systematic analysis of existing research into PBF globally (e.g., in Rwanda, Cambodia, Burundi) and the role and participation of African actors within global governance, with specific reference to South Africa, Tanzania, and Zambia. It involved content analysis of health strategies in South Africa, Tanzania, and Zambia; PBF directives and strategy documents of global and regional institutions such as WHO, World Bank, and the Global Fund; speeches and communications on PBF from the South African, Tanzanian, and Zambian Ministries of Health, Ministries of Finance, HIV/AIDS agencies, regional bodies; and reports and discussion documents on the role of PBF by southern African advocacy groups, civil society organisations, and the private sector. In the case of the Global Fund and World Bank, relevant PBF documents were freely accessible on-line via both institutional websites. These listed participating parties and delineated their specific functions, often providing contact details. The purpose of this policy and literature review was to identify events and institutions within the history of PBF development; develop a schematic map of diplomatic spaces and formal opportunities for participation within global health policy processes associated with the Global Fund and World Bank; and conduct a stakeholder analysis of the actors involved in policy deliberations, negotiations, and implementation

DOI: 10.1057/9781137500151.0005

of PBF (and any interconnections between them). The findings of such analysis are outlined in Figure 1.2. In addition, the literature and policy review revealed the rationale and preference of international donors implementing PBF, along with the role of southern African governments and civil society in conception, design, and implementation.

The schematic map outlined in Figure 1.2 and stakeholder analysis informed primary field research that was undertaken at the global and national level. The map and analysis were a means to (1) purposively identify key informants for interview in South Africa, Tanzania, and Zambia (including, for example, officials within central and regional government levels, Ministry of Finance, national HIV/AIDS agencies, health NGOs and advocacy groups, private sector partners, and external funders) and (2) identify possible formal meetings to observe. Importantly, to triangulate our interviews and to construct a more reliable and balanced understanding of participation in PBF, our team located groups outside the formal institutional process (i.e., outside health NGOs, regional political entities, civil groups, academics, and others affected or potentially affected by PBF initiatives).

The overall aim of the field research was to develop a detailed picture of how participation within PBF occurs, to trace the rationales associated with and practical application of PBF, and to explore how international donors and South African, Tanzanian, and Zambian actors experience and influence the conception, design, and delivery of PBF schemes. In total, 101 people participated in semi-structured interviews in the case study countries and the global health hubs of Washington, DC and Geneva. Interviews were either recorded and transcribed or captured through extensive note taking during the interview, with additional details added to the transcripts immediately after the interview. The interviews followed predesigned guidance questions related to PBF and the various participation mechanisms available. The questions were broadly divided into six parts. These were: (1) interviewee's professional association with PBF and background; (2) understanding of participation and partnership in global health; (3) understanding of PBF; (4) knowledge of decision-making processes; (5) influence on process; (6) contextual aspects of strategic planning, input, and outcomes of PBF. Interviewees gave oral or written informed consent to their participation and were fully informed of the research topic, intent to publish, and, where requested, able to confirm direct quotations. In addition, preliminary research findings were circulated to all research participants who

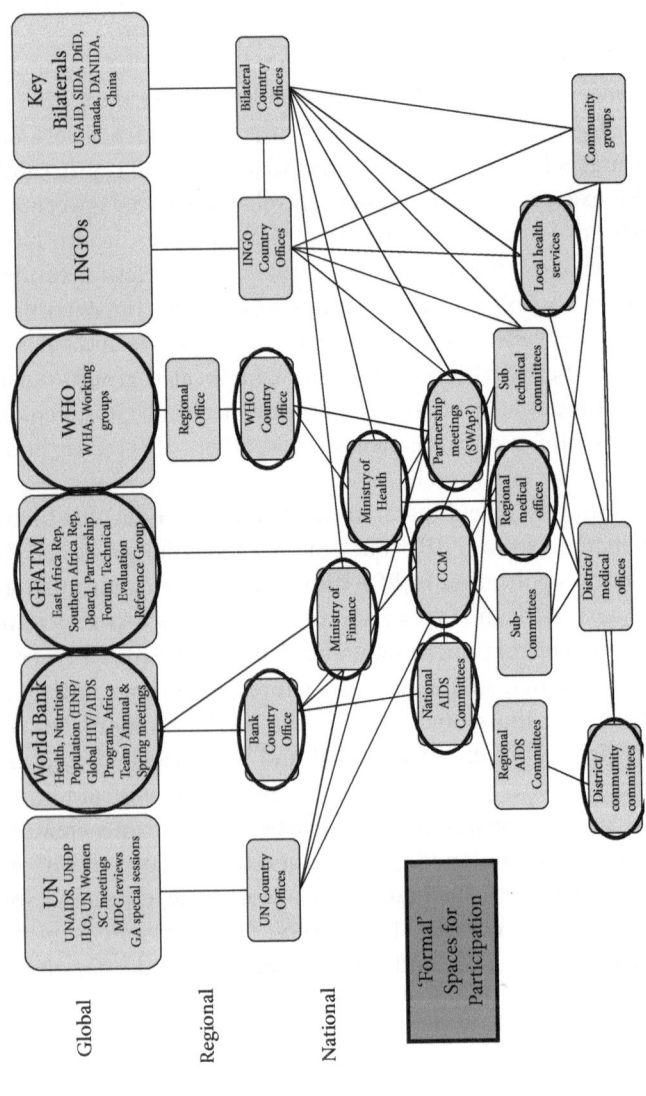

FIGURE 1.2 *Schematic diagram illustrating key diplomatic spaces for participating in global health policy processes*

DOI: 10.1057/9781137500151.0005

requested to see preliminary findings and participants were able to alter or withdraw their contribution at any point in the research process. All interviews are anonymised throughout the book.

The aim of the interviews in Washington, DC and Geneva was to investigate how global health institutions (particularly the World Bank and Global Fund) understand, rationalise, and seek to apply PBF, and to explore how this relates to national contexts of practice. The aim was also to explore more generally, from the perspective of global actors, what spaces exist for African actors to engage in global health policy processes. Interviews were conducted with 21 individuals based in the headquarters of the World Bank, Global Fund, WHO, UNAIDS, USAID, and Inter-American Development in both one-on-one and group settings.

The primary focus of interviews in the case study countries was to investigate how South African, Tanzanian, and Zambian actors are and/or have been involved in the conception, negotiation, design, and implementation of PBF initiatives involving global health institutions. Other international organisations were also engaged (i.e., USAID, DfID, CHAI). In South Africa, 24 people were interviewed, which were conducted in and around the areas of Cape Town, Johannesburg, and Pretoria. The interviewees represented a broad range of actors involved in the South African health system, including provincial and district health officials, the South African National AIDS Council, the Ministry of Health, the Department of Health, Treasury, Country Co-ordinating Mechanism (CCM) members, local consultants, principal recipients of Global Fund grants, UN agencies, East Central and Southern Africa Health Community, Southern African Development Community, and businesses involved in the health system. In Tanzania, 32 people were interviewed, this sample covered a broad range of actors involved in the health system. Interviewees included representatives of the Ministry of Health and Social Welfare, Ministry of Finance, UN agencies, World Bank, other external funder organisations, non-governmental organisations, and programme managers and principal recipients of Global Fund grants. In Zambia, 24 people were involved in interviews. These were representatives of external funding agencies, UN agencies, the Zambian CCM, principal recipients of the Global Fund, civil society organisations, the National HIV/AIDS Council, past Ministry of Health staff, and facility-level health workers in the Eastern Province.

Participant Observation of three key policy meetings was conducted in Tanzania. These meetings were the Annual Health Sector Review,

DOI: 10.1057/9781137500151.0005

October 2012; the Fifth P4P Advisory Committee, Ministry of Health and Social Welfare, October 2012; and the Joint Annual HIV/AIDS Technical Review, November 2012. Observation of these meetings demonstrated the practice of participation in formal meetings and allowed the research team to corroborate findings from interviews and provided follow-on lines of inquiry. In addition observation of care and treatment centres in the Pwani region of Tanzania was carried out in November 2012. The Pwani region is where the PBF pilot was taking place.

Analyses of the research data progressed by drawing on previous knowledge, experience, and existing literature about participation to triangulate, challenge, and reflect on the theoretical and practical implications of the findings. Interviews were analysed in an iterative way using thematic analysis (i.e., sorting/labelling/summarising data using predefined descriptive themes, such as understandings, assumptions, influences of process) while also identifying new, emergent ones. As the analysis progressed, higher level analytical themes were identified through a process of detecting patterns and developing explanations about participation and PBF in answering the research questions.

Structure of the book

The structure of the book is organised around four key research questions:

1   How have the concepts of participation and PBF emerged as key mechanisms of health reform in Africa?
2   How have different actors at different levels of governance participated in PBF processes in the World Bank and Global Fund?
3   What are the barriers to participation?
4   What is the role of African actors in shaping health reform in South Africa, Tanzania, and Zambia?

The book begins by answering the first two questions. Chapter 2 reviews what we know about PBF in global health governance. This chapter outlines the current debate and conceptual underpinnings surrounding PBF before focusing on some of the concerns and limitations of the PBF approach found in existing research. The chapter shows that despite such concerns the World Bank's HRITF continues to engage in the reproduction of a positive bias around PBF while obfuscating concerns as to the

DOI: 10.1057/9781137500151.0005

ways in which PBF can create health silos and lead to gaming around performance indicators.

Chapter 3 develops the argument established in Chapter 2 by exploring how PBF initiatives play out in practice in each of the three case studies. The chapter begins by outlining where PBF came from and the models of PBF adopted and how far advanced they are, for example, if they are at the pilot stage (Tanzania), being rolled out across the country (Zambia), or declining (South Africa). The chapter then reviews the positive gains made by PBF and why the initiative has gained such traction as a model for health system reform in Africa. Third, the chapter focuses on some of the direct and indirect outcomes associated with PBF that have potentially negative consequences for health system reform in South Africa, Tanzania, and Zambia. These issues are: the creation of health financing silos in the domestic and international health sectors; the politics of who sets the targets; and the practice of gaming the system. The chapter then reflects on changes to the governance of health brought about by PBF. This section of the chapter explores the role of consultants who broker relationships between government and donors and regulate the pace and timing of work of the health sector. In so doing, the chapter argues that PBF may not be the revolutionary tool of health system reform that is presented by international donors but another cumbersome and bureaucratic health policy fad that rests on a model of principal-agent theory complicated by multiple agents.

Chapter 4 builds on the previous two chapters by outlining what PBF initiatives tell us about participation in health policy formation. The chapter does so by first outlining how participation is understood in global health policy. Second, the chapter outlines the formal and informal spaces available for participation at the global, regional, and national level. In so doing it shows that while there are multiple spaces for formal participation, there is felt to be 'too much' of it within the health systems of South Africa, Tanzania, and Zambia at times. Third, the chapter considers a central issue associated with participation that is well-known to people working in the health systems of Tanzania and Zambia, but which is rarely discussed in academic literature on global health policy: paying for participation. Participation in meetings, workshops, and consultations often depends on per diems being paid to participants: without per diems participants often do not attend or prioritise other meetings because their attendance is not paid for. This per diem culture permeates the health systems of Tanzania and Zambia where per diems are of high value because of the amount of international aid that has concentrated in this area. This section of the chapter demonstrates how PBF exacerbates a per diem culture and the wider problem of 'the politics of the belly' (Bayart, 2012) in sub-Saharan Africa. The over-arching argument here is that productive participation happens in informal spaces and when participation is paid for. As a result, participation is skewed to favour elites who are familiar with informal spaces of engagement, and who are set to gain from performance and per diem financing in the health system. These gains to the elite lead to the reproduction of the idea that PBF is a positive health system intervention while at the same time silencing wider criticism of its negative externalities.

Chapter 5 brings together the main findings and conclusions of the book to argue that the theory and practice of participation and PBF remain tenuous, participatory processes of engagement in health reform are weakened, and African agency limited by the robustness of a health system and existing donor–recipient relations. Participation has become a somewhat empty concept that is based on payment and informal interactions rather than plurality of thought and ideas embedded into formal channels of wider communication and engagement. This is because participation and PBF operate within a market of global health policy where ideas are bought, sold, and marketed by international donors and governments, from which consultants also act as key brokers in such transactions. PBF and participation increasingly contribute to two-tier health systems comprised of those who are in the well-funded elite and those who work at the margins of health system reform. The chapter concludes by outlining four problems that the politics of participation and PBF demonstrate for health reform in Africa. With health reform back on the agenda, it is imperative that the issues outlined in this book are addressed in debate on the politics of health reform in Africa and for the successful realisation of the highest attainable standard of health for the African population.

DOI: 10.1057/9781137500151.0005

2

The Performance-Based Funding (PBF) Debate

Abstract: *This chapter outlines the main debate over results and performance-based funding (PBF) and the application of PBF to health system reform in Africa. It introduces the reader to principal–agent theory as the central approach to PBF adopted by the World Bank and Global Fund and outlines the many concerns and contentions associated with PBF. In so doing the chapter begins to show how global health institutions have adopted a positive bias to PBF as a tool for health system reform and that we know little about the role of African actors in the shaping and implementing of PBF programmes and in generating the evidence base that underpins them.*

Keywords: knowledge; results; PBF; positive bias; principal–agent theory

Barnes Amy, Garrett Wallace Brown and Sophie Harman. *Global Politics of Health Reform in Africa: Performance, Participation, and Policy.* Basingstoke: Palgrave Macmillan, 2015. DOI: 10.1057/9781137500151.0006.

Performance measurement has become an everyday part of contemporary life and is not unique to health system reform in Africa. Workers across the globe are managed by targets and assessment of outputs across various forms of employment; school children are given individualised goals for their educational attainment and performance; and consumers when presented with a range of products and services are required to rate their experience and the performance of the person who served them. Performance measurement has thus become a normalised part of the management and conduct of modern capitalist societies. The logic underpinning this everyday normality is that it increases efficiency and management of the workforce while ensuring that the consumer – whether of education, health care, holidays, or supermarket products – is the primary agent of concern. While this logic applies to the application of performance to health reform in Africa, the justification and use of performance-based funding (PBF) is grounded in a more revolutionary rhetoric of making health systems work in Africa. This chapter maps existing debate on PBF to introduce readers to what it is and how it is applied in practice, the contentions surrounding the application of PBF to health reform, and the gap in our understanding of how African actors participate in PBF design and implementation.

The PBF debate

Performance measurement and PBF have generated much research in the areas of sociology, economics, anthropology, international development, and public health. Debate on PBF in global health politics has been less developed and, on the whole, has been captured by research in development and health economics and by those donors that finance PBF, such as the World Bank's Health Results Innovation Trust Fund (HRITF) and the Global Fund. The debate in global health can generally be divided into two strands: (1) that which develops conceptual approaches to how PBF can be adopted and used effectively as a technical management tool; and (2) that which questions the evidence base and limitations of PBF approaches to health reform.

Conceptual approaches to PBF

The most often-cited conceptual approaches to PBF that have come to underpin the World Bank and Global Fund's programmes are grounded in a specific form of principal–agent theory. Principal–agent theory has been used by a range of scholars interested in performance programmes to explain the benefits of a contractual approach of PBF and the underlying mechanisms that link incentives to the delivery of pre-specified tasks (Eichler, 2006; Eldridge and Palmer, 2009; Ssengooba et al., 2012; Lawler, 1971; 1989). Principal–agent theory is used here to refer to the principal as the payer of particular desirable aspects of health service delivery or health outcomes. For example, the Global Fund, the government, or a non-governmental organisation (NGO) pays for the distribution of insecticide-treated nets (ITNs) to pregnant women. The agent is the provider or implementer, either an individual health worker or a health institution such as a hospital, clinic, or care and treatment centre. The principal pays the agent based on agreed results, or the achievement of particular performance criteria, targets, or indicators. In the example above, the agent could, for example, be paid based on them distributing an agreed number of ITNs. The logic here is that this type of contractual relationship elicits results in a setting where the principal cannot fully monitor the activities of the agent because of oversight problems such as bureaucracy and cost, but it is in the agent's financial interests to achieve the results and interests of the principal. As Eichler (2006) explains it, 'performance based reimbursement establishes explicit indicators of performance that are valued by the principal and provides financial and material incentives to agents for achieving defined performance targets'. The idea of PBF therefore relies on the assumption that agents are self-interested and motivated by financial gain, and will seek ways to maximise their income (Eldridge and Palmer, 2009). It also relies on a process of negotiating and agreeing a performance contract (upon which the principal–agent relationship is based), and a process of reporting and verification, whereby the principal can check and assess the agent's performance and achievement of results. In some cases, arbitration processes are necessary where there is disagreement about achieved results.

Based on such an approach, various frameworks have been constructed for the design and implementation of PBF. Eichler (2006) suggests a nine-step approach to PBF design, while Scheffler (2010) constructs a framework for the evaluation of PBF schemes which dually analyses the quality and efficiency of schemes. Common to these is a 'how-to' technical approach to PBF, offering practitioners a clear guide as to how PBF can be implemented and adapted to different country contexts. This is in

DOI: 10.1057/9781137500151.0006

part why such principal–agent frameworks have gained traction in the policy-making arena.

The dominance of principal–agent approaches has come into criticism for providing too much of a generalisable model that does not take context into consideration. This has led to a slight variant of such models: 'adaptive systems' or 'contingency' theory. These approaches to PBF illustrate and emphasise the impact that context has on programme implementation and therefore that implementation should take structural contexts into account. For example, PBF programmes must take into account bureaucratic structures, cultures, existing systems, and staffing, as these will all differ depending on the environment and institutional relationships in which PBF programmes are to be situated (Ssengooba et al., 2012; Leykum et al., 2007; Plsek and Wilson, 2001; Trisolini, 2011; Shortell and Kaluzny, 2006). Hence, this type of approach to PBF adopts the practical 'how-to' of principal–agent theory while adopting concepts such as ownership, cultural context, and institutional layers (Eldridge and Palmer, 2009; Trisolini, 2011; and Town et al., 2004) as a means of providing a context-structural fix within wider principal–agent frameworks.

Magrath and Nichter's (2012) anthropological approach to PBF offers an explicit acknowledgment of how structural differences impact and shape motivation. Magrath and Nichter draw on Bourdieu's (1977; 1986) 'habitus' framework to emphasise the importance of adaptation and context-specific PBF schemes. This framework distinguishes between economic, social, cultural, and symbolic capital as a means of demarcating how these forms of capital are acquired and converted from one form to another. For Magrath and Nichter, such a framework can be useful in explaining how PBF impacts on motivation depending on the design of funding schemes. The linkage here between habitus and motivation reveals how PBF intersects with existing power structures and reward systems and the access different actors have to these different types of capital within the schemes. In other words, the use of a habitus framework for analysis points to explaining how the key to PBF – motivation – works in practice in a variety of contexts and power structures. Identifying how motivation works and the structural constraints in which it operates is fundamental to the efficacy of PBF as a tool of health system reform.

Some studies have shown the success of PBF in improving process outcomes, for example, in increased access to, and utilisation of, priority

DOI: 10.1057/9781137500151.0006

health programmes and improvements in quality of care (Basinga et al., 2011; Brenzel et al., 2009; Soeters et al., 2006; Mamdani et al., 2012); and increased cost-effectiveness of health care at community and subnational levels (Fryatt et al., 2010). Many authors argue that PBF can have a positive impact on the strengthening of health systems and their governance, as well as local participation in the design and implementation of funding schemes. For instance, Meessen et al. (2011) counter-critique those that focus too much on PBF as a method of payment rather than as a source of health system reform. They argue that because PBF schemes form contractual relationships rather than hierarchical ones, each organisational unit involved in the process must account for their performance, and, as a result, accountability and efficiency should increase. Levine and Oomman (2009) see PBF as a way to overcome issues associated with resource pooling due to an overwhelming concentration of health care funding towards HIV/AIDS programmes, by setting targets that strengthen health systems in general. Where criticism exists in these studies, it is with regard to how to make PBF more technical and work better, not a critique of the appropriateness of the model itself. As a consequence the favourable conclusions in such reports (Low-Beer et al., 2007; Meessen et al., 2011) tend to be adopted and used as justification for PBF by institutions such as the World Bank and Global Fund. The concern here is that this adoption can often be at the exclusion of other more critical or non-favourable PBF evidence.

Tensions and criticism of PBF

Positive research on PBF is contentious precisely because it has been used by global health institutions to justify further investment in this approach to health system reform in Africa, while obfuscating those studies that highlight its limitations (Ireland et al., 2011). Such contention points to a second important part of the literature on the PBF debate: that which questions the evidence base and justification for further investment, and the tendency towards a positive approach to PBF by policy-makers. For some, in terms of the actual impacts of PBF, the current evidence base does not sufficiently support the widespread implementation of PBF schemes (Eijkenaar et al., 2013). Even where evidence has indicated improvements in specific or narrow outputs, an inability to isolate key variables that determine the effects of PBF as well as a lack of research control groups means that these effects cannot be solely attributed to PBF

(Eijkenaar et al., 2013; Eldridge and Palmer, 2009; Mæstad, 2007; Witter et al., 2012). For example, a study by Basinga et al. (2011) – widely cited and one of the more convincing empirical studies of the impact of PBF in low- and middle-income countries – showed target-specific benefits of PBF schemes in Rwanda, but not why those benefits came about. Montagu and Yamey (2011) highlight that even where PBF has led to increases in quantity and quality of care, this does not necessarily translate into increased population health, a view echoed by Eldridge and Palmer (2009). Meeting a target under a PBF strategy does not necessarily equate to an improvement in health outcomes or in the overall health system. Indeed, there is a clear lack of evaluations of the long-term impact that PBF schemes have on health outcomes (Eijkenaar et al., 2013). As a consequence, the evidence base supporting PBF is often branded as inconclusive, flawed, or low in quality (Emmert et al., 2012; Eijkenaar et al., 2013; Eldridge and Palmer, 2009; Ireland et al., 2011; Magrath and Nicther, 2012; Montagu and Yamey, 2011; Scheffler, 2010; Witter et al., 2012).

Some studies on PBF have predicted or observed initial indications of unintended consequences of PBF strategies, with potential short- and long-term detrimental effects on health service provision. Among the concerns raised, it is suggested that PBF can distort the priorities of national health systems due to targeting of services (Ireland et al., 2011; Scheffler, 2010); lead to 'gaming', false reporting of results, and 'cherry-picking' of patients (Ireland et al., 2011; Kalk, 2011); give rise to 'perverse incentives' (Fryatt et al., 2010); lead to a focus on quantity over quality of service (Ireland et al., 2011; Langenbrunner and Liu, 2005); perpetuate in-country inequities by targeting areas where targets are more easily met (Ireland et al., 2011); and carry debilitating hidden costs for establishing and monitoring PBF systems (Kalk, 2011). Trisolini (2011) and Cockerham (2007) raise concerns that the increased involvement of multiple non-medical actors in health-care provision often associated with PBF mechanisms can demotivate health professionals due to fears of de-professionalisation of the field, with negative consequences for care practices. Specifically in relation to Global Fund PBF schemes, based on data from 508 Global Fund grants, Fan et al. (2013) argue that by virtue of calculating grants using a multitude of indicators and discretionary factors, 'the incentives transmitted from the Global Fund to its recipients are weak at best' (Fan et al., 2013: e166). If recipients do not see how performance is tied to future disbursement of grants, or they view the Fund's calculating mechanism as inaccurate, they are unlikely to be incentivised to achieve set goals (ibid.).

DOI: 10.1057/9781137500151.0006

Others have argued that generalised conclusions were drawn from case studies that use exceedingly varied methods of PBF and were undertaken in disparate settings that are too varied to draw such conclusions (Witter et al., 2012), resulting in a failure to appreciate the causes of effects of PBF, rather than their magnitude (Ssengooba et al., 2012).

What this dense review of the literature suggests is that PBF is not without its well-known and well-researched flaws. However, despite such flaws, researchers such as Ireland et al. (2011) note a favourable bias towards PBF among policy makers and scholars, which has led to the overlooking of negative consequences and the sweeping attribution of positive outcomes to PBF schemes with limited consideration of other factors. This view is clearly supported by the website of the World Bank's HRITF, which is a comprehensive store of research and publications on various forms of PBF (see HRITF, 2014b). In particular, the RBF Health blog (previously called the 'All things RBF' blog) is revealing in the positive bias attributed to performance approaches to health system reform. None of the 38 blog entries published as of July 2014 were overtly critical or specific about potential limitations of PBF. One entry from May 2013 addressed some of the concerns raised about pay-for-performance and then systematically dismissed them (Friedman, 2013). Four entries outlined some of the challenges with successful implementation of the project, for example, the problems of bottlenecks in the health system (Meessen, 2013), the need to ensure usage of voucher schemes by the beneficiaries (Tannis, 2014), and the need to avoid health silos by matching targets to existing country Health Management Information Systems data (de Borman, 2014). However, these challenges were weighed against an extensive list of the advantages to PBF in each of these entries and, in some cases, stories of successes from PBF flagship countries such as Rwanda, Burundi, and Benin. One particularly revealing challenge noted by a health officer working in Zimbabwe was the need to separate 'the program from politics, and maintaining a truly apolitical reputation' (Mlambo, 2014). All of the 38 blog entries stressed the positive aspects of PBF, noting the 'transformative power' of PBF to make health systems accountable, effective, and strategic. Such a positive bias is unsurprising given the amount of money the World Bank has invested in these programmes as flagships of its Health, Nutrition, and Population section and some of the positive gains arising from the project. However, the use of PBF-friendly bloggers – implementing partner NGOs such as Cordaid, World Bank consultants, and representatives from 'success story' country health ministries – and the lack of representation of some of the limitations of or potential alternatives to PBF – and of those who are more hesitant about its transformative power – reinforce the positive bias. The type of research, bloggers, and positive bias reflect a pattern of the World Bank seemingly underplaying criticisms of or problems with the PBF approach to reform that we will see further in Chapters 3 and 4. This begins to show us that participants involved in the shaping of PBF within the Bank tend to be those that are on board with the 'success story', framing PBF as a transformational model of health system reform.

Participation and PBF

The concept of 'participation' underpins much of the thinking surrounding the idea of PBF. Low-Beer et al. (2007: 1309) state, for example, that 'performance-based funding is based on radical country ownership of targets and implementation'. Other studies highlight the importance of participation to the PBF process. Eldridge and Palmer (2009) draw parallels between PBF and donor conditionality in the 1980s and the failures of the Bretton Woods institutions in this area. They argue that the lack of national control of the schemes exhibited at the time provides important lessons for PBF about the way country-level actors are engaged. Other studies similarly emphasise that participation and local ownership of the process is vital for the successful implementation of PBF schemes. First, autonomy for health providers and other local stakeholders in preparing and implementing schemes is important as it encourages entrepreneurial spirit, leads to better human resource management, and increases collaboration with the private sector, all of which enhance performance (Toonen et al., 2009; Soeters et al., 2006). Second, funding must be aligned with the priorities of recipient governments and stakeholders. National ownership ensures schemes are embedded within overarching strategies rather than isolated in a vertical approach (Levine and Oomman, 2009; Toonen et al., 2009). Third, PBF schemes require institutional and political support which can only be achieved if partners at all levels of operationalisation within health systems are involved in identifying problems, priorities, and strategies to address these (Oxman and Fretheim, 2009; Toonen et al., 2009).

However, there is a distinct lack of scholarship on actual participation in the decision-making processes related to PBF. It is less evident how such country ownership is reproduced by PBF strategies and how different actors set the agenda for PBF, its application and evaluation. There is

DOI: 10.1057/9781137500151.0006

no systematic research on the relationship between PBF and participation, and how African actors have participated in the design, implementation, and delivery of PBF initiatives on the continent. In addition, there is limited empirical research to determine whether negotiations and deliberations have been equitable, and what implications this has in terms of reshaping local forms of governance, participation, and authority. This is a curious intellectual gap given that much of the rationale behind PBF is that it works effectively if local ownership of the process is maintained, as highlighted above. As will be presented in the chapters that follow, due to the nature of World Bank and Global Fund PBF mechanisms, most participation takes place unilaterally between the funder and the national government/principal recipients. This often does not involve regional actors and tends to exclude and/or undervalue many local stakeholders; although this varies from case to case and is primarily determined by how well stakeholders are incorporated into decision-making processes by national bodies during wider prioritisation/target-setting processes, or specific grant/loan writing stages.

African actors within national governments generally *participate* in the design, implementation, and evaluation of PBF schemes, even if the *quality* of that participation, including their ability to negotiate PBF schemes, may vary. This raises questions about how much influence or power is being exerted and how much freedom of action African political actors have available to them within global and national health policy formation and implementation. Simply put, while we are aware of the debate surrounding PBF, we do not know the extent to which these concerns are shared by those involved in the implementation of such strategies, whether such actors align with the positive bias towards PBF as a source of health reform, or if their concerns as agents have been silenced by the principals that fund them. We do not know if African actors asked for PBF, if PBF is applied differently in different African health systems, or if participation in the design and implementation of PBF strategies is equitable between African governments, civil society, health professionals, and their development partners.

Conclusion

This short chapter has provided an overview of the debate surrounding PBF in global health system reform. In so doing it has presented the

DOI: 10.1057/9781137500151.0006

framework of principal–agent models of reform that the World Bank and Global Fund adopt in their PBF projects and the extensive misgivings of such an approach outlined in existing research. The chapter has highlighted the positive bias in how PBF research is used by the World Bank as justification for expanding this approach to health reform and the lack of recognition of how African actors have participated in the shaping and implementation of PBF programmes in African countries. In so doing, this chapter has begun to show that there is a politics to how knowledge about PBF is used and a gap in our understanding as to how African actors participate in the reproduction and use of such knowledge. The next chapter develops these findings by looking at the wider politics of PBF and its application to health reform in South Africa, Tanzania, and Zambia.

DOI: 10.1057/9781137500151.0006

3

The Politics of Performance-Based Funding (PBF)

Abstract: *This chapter introduces the reader to how performance-based funding (PBF) works in practice in South Africa, Tanzania, and Zambia and where the idea for PBF came from. In so doing it reviews how health workers in these countries understand PBF, the problems associated with implementing PBF and its multiple levels of governance, and the origins of PBF as a health reform tool. The chapter shows evidence of discontent towards PBF in South Africa and how a positive bias is reproduced by donors in Tanzania and Zambia through the promise of finance and study tours to 'success story' countries. The chapter outlines the role of consultants and international agencies, which increasingly have a brokerage role in global health governance that challenges the practical application of the principal–agent model of PBF.*

Keywords: consultants; bureaucracy; PBF; positive bias; principal–agent brokers; south-south learning

Barnes Amy, Garrett Wallace Brown and Sophie Harman. *Global Politics of Health Reform in Africa: Performance, Participation, and Policy.* Basingstoke: Palgrave Macmillan, 2015. DOI: 10.1057/9781137500151.0007.

The confidence in performance-based funding (PBF) as a transformative tool of health system reform in Africa put forward by international institutions and individuals working in 'success story' countries such as Burundi and Rwanda, and the rational, practical, even boring, method in which it is supposed to enact reform, would suggest there is not much of a politics to it. As Chapter 2 has shown, most criticism of PBF has been about its technical limitations and questionable efficacy and evidence base. However, our research shows that there is a clear politics to the understanding of PBF, how the idea for PBF as a tool of health system reform came about, and who participates (and who does not) in shaping the 'success story' model of PBF reform. The aim of this chapter is to show that there is a politics to PBF with regard to where the idea came from, the traction it has gained as a panacea to problems of African health system reform, the burden it places on health systems and officials, and how South Africa is challenging whether the costs outweigh the benefits of such an approach.

The chapter fulfils this aim by first outlining what PBF looks like in South Africa, Tanzania, and Zambia and how different actors understand PBF. Second, the chapter explores the origins of PBF and investigates current arguments that suggest that such an approach can be taken as evidence of African agency and 'south-to-south learning'. Third, the chapter explores the problem of consultants as brokers and also the role of elites in the creation and maintenance of the PBF success story and the exclusionary limits to participation such actors create. It then moves on to explore the problem of health silos, confusion, and gaming that can occur as a consequence of PBF, which has led some health officials to question whether PBF is worth pursuing as it is currently propagated. Fourth, the chapter questions the evidence base for PBF before drawing together its conclusions.

PBF reform in South Africa, Tanzania, and Zambia

There are two main types of PBF programme that are being applied to health system reform in South Africa, Tanzania, and Zambia. These are depicted in Table 3.1. The first type, 'Type I', is a straightforward results-based system (as called in Zambia and South Africa) or pay-for-performance (P4P) programme (as called in Tanzania) in which health professionals (doctors, laboratory technicians, ambulance drivers) or the

DOI: 10.1057/9781137500151.0007

TABLE 3.1 *Typical features of the two broad types of PBF*

Type	Types of performance target	Level of action within health system	Examples of targets	Notes/Issues	Donor
I	Narrow targets based on payment for service/outputs	Often district or facility based and/or may be targeted at individual health professionals	Number of pregnant women counselled and tested for HIV; number of HIV pregnant women given Nevirapine or AZT; number of fully vaccinated children under one year of age; number of institutional deliveries; antenatal care (ANC), prenatal and follow-up visits	Easier to set targets/ track performance	Global Fund World Bank
II	Targets based on broader health system indicators/ outcomes	Often national/ health system based and targeted at whole Ministry of Health or similar health-related department	Health workers by 1,000 population (HMIS); total health expenditure per capita (HMIS); proportion of births attended by skilled personnel (MDG); prevalence of underweight children under five years of age (MDG)	Local pressure to integrate PBF into system strengthening; reliable targets hard to set due to M & E shortcomings/ difficult to track performance	Global Fund

DOI: 10.1057/9781137500151.0007

TABLE 3.2 *Key features of the 'Type I – Fee for Service' PBF programmes in Tanzania and Zambia*

Features	Tanzania	Zambia
Overview	Provision of fee-for-service incentive payments based on individual and institutional performance	Provision of fee-for-service incentive payments based on individual and institutional performance
Aim/focus	Maternal and child health – To accelerate the attainment of MDGs 4 and 5	Maternal and child health – To increase coverage of maternal/child services (and improve outcomes) in rural areas by changing behaviour/system strengthening
External support	CHAI with the Norwegian Ministry of Foreign Affairs	World Bank (through HRITF) with particular support from Norwegian Ministry of Foreign Affairs – HRITF US$16.79 million (initial grant was US$12 million)
Geographic focus	Pwani region – seven districts	Initially implemented in Katete district. Larger pilot now involves 10 districts across provinces (Mumbwa, Lufwanyama, Lundazi, Mwense, Mporokoso, Isoka, Mufumbwe, Siavonga, Senanga)
Stakeholders	All facilities (hospitals, health centres, dispensaries) within the seven districts are eligible to participate if they provide reproductive and child health services, have full HMIS data, and have bank accounts. Supervising authorities at district and regional levels are eligible for bonuses (district Council Health Management Teams and Regional Health Management Team)	Health facilities with one trained health worker are eligible. Neighbourhood health committees intended to support community participation in decision-making process. District- and provincial-level structures have supervisory/governance roles: performance assessment (either of facilities or districts), audit, technical support and coordination of activities. Stakeholders at national level are the MoH HQ (incl. Project Implementation Unit) and National RBF Steering Committee

Targets and indicators	6 monthly bonus payments based on maternal and child health service indicators, HMIS strengthening, facility management, and overall performance. Examples of facility indicators: proportion of antenatal clients on malaria prophylaxis; proportion of newly delivered mothers who attended postnatal clinic within 7 days. Other indicators linked to bonuses at facilities: % of HIV+ clients on ARVs for prevention of mother-to-child transmission; proportion of facility-based deliveries. Correct/correctly used partographs as hospital indicator	Pre-agreed core package of nine facility-based indicators associated with extra payments: curative consultations, institutional deliveries by skilled birth attendant, ANC prenatal and follow-up visits, postnatal visit, full immunisation of children under 1 year of age, pregnant women receiving 3 doses of malaria IPT, FP users of modern methods at the end of the month, pregnant women counselled and tested for HIV, no. of HIV pregnant women given Nevirapine+ and AZT
Judgement of performance	Performance score calculations submitted. Overall performance score calculations made. Planned and random checks by various verifiers. (NB: Implementation is accompanied by introduction of new HMIS designed to strengthen collection/use of HMIS data)	Indicator index and associated fee schedule. Verifications through monthly quantity audits and quarterly quality audits. Performance calculated by multiplying a quality score with the total quantity of services delivered (based on nine indicators)
Payments	Every 6 months. Facility bonus paid for disbursement to staff and for facility operations (maximum $723 in dispensaries and $7,875 in hospitals). Staff top ups can be 10% of monthly salary for maternal/child health workers	Quarterly. Health facilities divide payments based on staff performance bonuses (based on a staff index) and can use payments for reinvestment (min. 25% of total): e.g, to buy drugs, recruit temporary nurses and midwives
Other information		To trigger demand for services, incentives (in kind or cash) are provided to traditional birth attendants, pregnant mothers, undernourished children

Sources: Borghi et al. (2013); HRITF (2013); MoH (Zambia) (2011).

DOI: 10.1057/9781137500151.0007

health facility in which they work get paid when they meet certain outputs or outcomes related to service delivery. This is usually in the form of a bonus payment and performance tends to be identified by a set of indicators articulated by international donors or drawn from national Health Management Information Systems (HMIS) data. So, for example, in relation to HIV this could involve assessment of performance in relation to the number of pregnant women counselled and tested for HIV or the number of HIV pregnant women given AZT. As indicated in Chapter 1, this type of project is at the preliminary pilot stage in Tanzania (supported by the Clinton Health Access Initiative, CHAI), and the advanced pilot stage in Zambia (supported by the World Bank through the Health Results Innovation Trust Fund, HRITF). Both pilots focus on indicators based on outputs or outcomes for maternal and newborn child health and these tend to be either tied to HIV/AIDS or malaria. As Table 3.2 suggests, some targets are linked to individual health workers, while others are based on the health centre or clinic as the delivery agent. On the other side of the principal–agent relationship, each case involves a complex combination of international donors and government agencies that make up the principal. Country-based consultants are also involved in the pilots, either working within Tanzanian and Zambian government ministries or with the international agencies such as CHAI and the World Bank. The consultants often act as brokers within the PBF process, for example, delivering training for agents and/or verifying progress for principals. In South Africa, there are preliminary discussions and initial work, particularly within the national treasury (with ongoing talks with the World Bank) around introducing Type I PBF frameworks for hospitals and health professionals as part of South Africa's National Health Strategic Plan (NSP), but these are currently at an early stage of development.

The 'Type II' PBF framework (see Table 3.1) aligns more closely with older models of aid conditionality: whereby broader and sometimes system-wide objectives, indicators, and targets are set by national recipients of aid (with external funder input in many cases), and as long as targets are met (or nearly met), the money keeps coming. The slight, but vital, shift is that recipients of aid often have to demonstrate results with their own funds before receiving money and/or consistently do not receive any further funds if the agreed targets are not met. This type of PBF programme is being widely introduced to HIV/AIDS funding and other areas of health financing by agencies such as the Global Fund and

DOI: 10.1057/9781137500151.0007

the United States Agency for International Development (USAID), and through sector budget support.

As indicated in Chapter 1, Global Fund projects are in operation in all three of the case study countries and tend to contain both Type I and Type II performance targets. For example, in relation to the Global Fund's health system strengthening component, the service readiness score for health facilities and facilities reporting no stock-out of antimalarial, tuberculosis (TB), and antiretroviral (ARV) drugs would be considered examples of Type 1 targets, and the percentage of births attended by professional health providers and child mortality examples of Type II targets (see Global Fund, 2011a). As with all Global Fund projects, grant applications are made by a principal recipient (PR) in conjunction with a locally organised multi-sectoral body – the Country Co-ordination Mechanism (CCM). CCMs are made up of a combination of government agencies, civil society actors, and private sector stakeholders and are supposed to oversee Global Fund operations, manage and disburse grants to PRs, and liaise with the Global Fund in Geneva. The PR is responsible for delivery and reporting, but can contract delivery roles out to sub-recipients (SRs). A local fund agent (LFA) (usually an international accountancy firm) is responsible for checking and verifying performance and results.

In Tanzania, the CCM is called the Tanzania National Coordinating Mechanism (TNCM) and is hosted by the Tanzania Commission for AIDS (TACAIDS). The TNCM coordinates other funding sources beyond that of the Global Fund (TACAIDS, 2014). In Zambia, the CCM is a relatively autonomous body, but the CCM Secretariat is housed within the National HIV/AIDS/STI/TB Council (NAC). In South Africa, a complicated Global Fund system exists, in which there are provincial CCMs (Western Cape) and a national CCM under the organisation and chairmanship of the South African National AIDS Council (SANAC). Although the provincial and national CCMs have in the past operated independently, there has been recent movement to unify health delivery in South Africa under the NSP, and SANAC now has the mandate to lead in all future Global Fund grant initiatives. As will be discussed later, this has caused a certain level of apprehension from non-governmental organisations (NGOs) and provincial PRs who remain sceptical of SANAC due to its past inability to coordinate grants. In addition, ongoing grants (Western Cape) are still locked into unilateral arrangements with

DOI: 10.1057/9781137500151.0007

the Fund until grant closure in 2016 and thus continue to independently implement, monitor, and report on their grant.

The aim of the Global Fund model is to create nationally owned projects and associated targets that best fit the specialised needs of a particular country, province, or group. The choice of project and performance targets and indicators is left to the relevant CCM to decide. The Global Fund Secretariat in Geneva does, however, recommend particular output and outcome indicators for consideration (see Global Fund, 2011a; 2011b: 223), which shapes local discussions. This influencing effect and, indeed, the entire model complicate the idea of principal–agent relationships within PBF. In theory, the Secretariat in Geneva, in partnership with the relevant country-based CCM, should be the principal and the PR the agent – who is motivated to deliver and perform. In effect, however, a complex and overlapping system of principal–agent relationships is set up. PRs contract with SRs and so become both a principal and an agent. Furthermore, the LFA encroaches on the principal–agent relationship, since it not only brokers within the process, verifying what agents are doing, but in so doing also increasingly takes on a principal role in the system, which effectively skews lines of accountability and responsibility. This confusion is compounded by the role of the Technical Review Panel (TRP), which scrutinises grant proposals from the CCMs in order to make funding recommendations to the Global Fund Board. These issues reflect a practical flaw in the Global Fund's theoretical system of PBF because it sets up multiple principals and agents at multiple levels of health system governance. This is a fundamental frustration of the principal–agent model and, as will be explained below (and in the next chapter), results in confusion and complex bureaucracy.

How do different actors understand PBF?

The World Bank, USAID, the Global Fund, WHO, and African stakeholders in Geneva and Washington, DC generally believed that PBF serves three overall policy functions in South Africa, Tanzania, and Zambia. First, that PBF is a mechanism to better monitor health interventions so that more reliable evidentiary judgements could be made about what policies work and what policies struggle to generate results. As one Global Fund interviewee claimed, PBF 'ensures that funding decisions are based on transparent assessment of results' (Interview GEN1). In this regard, despite a lack of correlative evidence to suggest that PBF produces significantly better health outcomes, most respondents made a firm link between PBF mechanisms and global initiatives to increase evidence-based policy. Second, there was a unanimous belief that PBF either limited corruption or was a mechanism designed by external funders to help curb corruption by increasing the level of accountability by recipients. As one country health attaché to the UN suggested, 'they want to make sure their [funders] money isn't buying new BMWs for the minister' (Interview GEN2). Third, and related, PBF was seen as a mechanism to increase value for money and limit waste. As one country delegate to the WHO suggested, 'The logic behind these funding models is to get more from the money spent and to make sure the money is going to the right places' (Interview GEN3).

Members of the Global Fund stressed their belief that PBF is about being accountable to those most in need by only funding projects that 'impacted on people's well-being in measurable and meaningful ways' (Interview GEN4). However, this view was not always shared by country representatives in Geneva, who often suggested that accountability was hierarchical at the Global Fund with priority given to the demands of the funders (as principals in the PBF process). Beyond these core policy functions, a large number of respondents were keen to stress the wider functions of PBF for health system reform. As one representative of USAID commented:

> What I like about PBF, is it is a systematic approach to strengthening health systems.... It strengthens the health system because it strengthens all the WHO building blocks, it really attacks, addresses each one of them and tries to improve them and I think this is a powerful, potentially powerful intervention to do that. It's a lot more than pay for performance. (Interview WAS1)

For those working on the implementation of PBF in South Africa, Tanzania, and Zambia, PBF was seen less as a tool of health system reform. Instead, PBF was deemed to be broadly about showing and checking results, and about accountability (to external funders): you propose to do something and hit certain targets, and then you get the money when you show performance. This is illustrated in the following excerpts from interviews in Tanzania and Zambia.

> With PBF you have to, for example if you want to give me money, you want me to use whatever I have and then I show you I have managed. This is my plan. I plan to provide services to this number of people, and this is my budget. Let's say $1,000, I need $1,000 to provide for 100 people. Now I depend on you to give me money, but you don't want to give me money straight, but you want

to show, to look for some resources, if I get like $500 or $600, up to $1,000 I need. I do some work with $600 and then I report to you that I have managed to secure $600 out of my targets but this is not enough and then what you do – correct me if I am wrong – what you do is if you see that I have made some efforts and I have given the milestones, I have done this, you say okay if that is what you have done I give you the dollars. And then another quarter or another year then you support me. (Interview TNZ1)

Okay broadly that whatever financing you're going to give me, I'll only merit more finances as I give feedback. And feedback based on what we have agreed will be the measure and we call it performance. (Interview TNZ2)

... results-based financing is really funding programmes according to how they perform, or according to a set target or according to, so you can either say if you reach this target I will give you this amount or for every to provide, I will give you this amount. (Interview ZAM1)

What is notable here is the positive stance taken towards PBF, or at least the potential of PBF by both international donors and their African partners. In general, most of the country-level respondents in South Africa, Tanzania, and Zambia were positive about the need to reform how health financing works and to make it more accountable to donors and users, and those in Zambia and Tanzania were pleased to see money going towards maternal and child health. These respondents saw PBF as shining a light on where money in the health system goes and making those working in the health system more responsible. Government officials working in HIV/AIDS councils were also positive, but were worried about funds being deflected away from HIV/AIDS as a result. Transparency, motivation, autonomy, and alignment with the rest of the world were all cited as positive factors by key in-country stakeholders.

Those actors that understand PBF – what it is, how it works, and its intent – tended to be those directly involved in its implementation. In Zambia and Tanzania, those with the clearest understanding or familiarity with the term were the principal recipients of Global Fund grants, external funders themselves, or working in government who were piloting P4P or PBF programmes. In South Africa, however, all interviewees seemed familiar with the idea of PBF and appeared content to use the term in discussing the South African health system. When asked, most civil society organisations and government officials interviewed in Tanzania and Zambia were reticent to say what they thought PBF was, who is doing it, and how it is applied, as they were not particularly familiar with PBF as a particular term. For example, one respondent in Zambia suggested:

DOI: 10.1057/9781137500151.0007

We do not have performance-based financing. I mean well maybe yes and no. Let me say yes and no. I think the US component is the fact that all these projects you get funding only after you submit your reports and satisfactory report and the next trunk of money comes, even the project we have with CHAI, they only give us the funding after certain deliverables....

So that is performance based funding?

(Laughing) Yeah. (Interview ZAM2)

Some interviewees appeared to be more conversant with other terms used to signify this type of funding modality. Terminology was a major determinant of understanding; for example, a doctor working in a health centre that was part of the P4P pilot in Tanzania was familiar with the term P4P but had not heard of PBF more broadly or with a detailed understanding of PBF as a reform tool. This supports a recent study by Ifakara Health Institute (2013), which suggested the existence of broader uncertainly about PBF mechanisms in Tanzania, highlighting that 'after two years of the pilot, most stakeholders did not know what P4P was' (Interview TNZ3). Understanding of PBF was therefore mixed: most actors working in the health sector knew roughly what it was about and how it works; however, the revolutionary potential of PBF as a tool of health reform was an understanding mainly held by donors, not those working in the systems to be reformed.

Where did PBF as a tool of health reform in Africa come from?

Further to different understandings of what the purpose of PBF is, there was some discrepancy among donors, African government officials, and civil society as to where the idea for it came from. International institutions such as the WHO and health-related UN bodies recognised PBF's roots in new public management approaches to policy reform of the 1990s. Some individuals working in the WHO and the Global Fund cited PBF as coming from educational reform models in the United States in the 1970s. The majority of WHO and UN interviewees understood PBF as an international donor-driven initiative. In particular, it was widely believed that most large bilateral agencies were strongly pushing the adoption of PBF financing models and that this was further pursued by health consultants working for these agencies. For example, one African member of the Joint United Nations Programme on AIDS (UNAIDS) suggested:

DOI: 10.1057/9781137500151.0007

> Organisations like Gates, Clinton and USAID are suggesting PBF as an effective health reform tool…there are a great deal of consultants and experts brought in to discuss things and I think they are keen on the idea of PBF. (Interview GEN5)

Another WHO delegate remarked:

> On the whole, donors and consultants are in favour of target driven financing and they have successfully entrenched this as the primary mode of operation. (Interview GEN3)

A representative for Africa in WHO furthered stated:

> Funders are the main proponents of PBF and this is often made very clear in WHO policy conversations…[so] there is not much scope for discussing funding modalities in the WHO…. I mean it does come up, but more in terms of the system needing targeted aid, and more of it. We largely discuss policy in terms of priorities, strategy and practice, not on the details of aid delivery. (Interview GEN6)

However, the externally driven thesis for the origins of PBF as a tool of health reform in Africa was challenged by respondents from the World Bank who suggested that African countries had been clearly demanding such an intervention within health systems for a long time. Indeed, the Bank was particularly keen to stress the African origins of the project. As one World Bank staff member indicated, 'the demand is overwhelming, we have a very hard time meeting the demands [for PBF]' (Interview WAS2).

Rwanda was presented as an integral component to the African-origins thesis of PBF. In interviews, Rwanda was consistently cited by World Bank staff and also individuals familiar with PBF from civil society and the donor community (such as USAID and CHAI) as the key originator of PBF as a tool of health reform in Africa. As one Bank staff member noted:

> We as an institution, we have learned a lot from, and we continue to learn a lot from the collective experience in Rwanda…this shift from an input based approach to an outcome-based approach. And Rwanda pioneered many things in that regard. (Interview WAS3)

It is not only the World Bank that learns from Rwanda however: the Bank has facilitated workshops and study tours to PBF 'success story' countries such as Rwanda and Burundi by other African countries, including Tanzania and Zambia. As one World Bank interviewee explained:

They usually organise by themselves study tours or we finance it, to see it, to visit a neighbouring country to visit it, and see how a design works and then they sort of embark on a process where they adapt the general idea to a local context. (Interview WAS2)

Here, these PBF study tours were presented as a unique form of south-to-south learning, given that the most common form has in the past been between Brazil, China, India, and African countries (Interview WAS4). Mutual knowledge exchange between African countries could therefore be seen as a distinctly claimed space for the participation of African actors in global health policy processes.

The tension over where the idea for PBF as a tool of health reform originated is complicated, however, by the perception of PBF origins in South Africa, Tanzania, and Zambia. Key stakeholders in these three countries acknowledged external donor pressure to adopt PBF models, but downplayed the role of Rwanda, each stressing that they had in some way adopted PBF long before the Rwanda 'success story' or the Global Fund. This was particularly the case in South Africa and Zambia. In each of the three countries there is a complex history of PBF that showed previous attempts at performance-based health reform and a push and pull between the type and scale of PBF reform each government wanted and that particular donors would be willing to fund.

This push and pull is perhaps most clearly evident in the confused history of PBF in Tanzania. Initially the government had wanted a country-wide PBF intervention rolled out in the area of MNCH (Maternal Newborn Child Health) as the government did not favour pilots (Interview TNZ4). Respondents attributed this to pilot fatigue and a commitment to universalism across the country by the government of Tanzania. However, international donors wanted to pilot the project first. It was also reported that negotiations between the government, the World Bank, CHAI, and Norway meant that this ended up being channelled into a parallel programme. As one interviewee explained:

The original model of P4P was meant to be built on a joint basket with money from Norway. However, the World Bank demanded that P4P funds could not be from a joint basket and thus forced a parallel funding mechanism to be designed. (Interview TNZ3)

After on-off discussions and something of a stalemate, CHAI brokered a partnership with the government for a pilot to take place in the Pwani region. This pilot was only meant to be short term before a country-wide

DOI: 10.1057/9781137500151.0007

scale up; however, there were delays in this happening. As a result, there is frustration on the part of some consultants to the Ministry of Health and Social Welfare (MoHSW) that this is not really being taken seriously (Interview TNZ5). This is perhaps an unfair classification of those directly involved in the project that showed commitment to making it a success. However, in practice they are running in parallel to existing operations in the MoHSW, with the only people really aware of their activities being those working on MNCH at the national level and in Pwani. Research observations revealed that the pilot was not flagged at the 2012 Annual Health Sector Review in any real depth, and some respondents implied that this was just another external funder fad. Clearly, this explanation contradicts the supposition that PBF is an example of south–south participation and learning; the design and conception of PBF is actually far more politically complex. This history has led to many different interpretations of where PBF originated. For example, people working in the health sector in Tanzania noted:

> I'm not sure but definitely it did not originate in this country, but literature tells us it has been piloted in many countries. I've not searched very much the literature but I think we saw here about 4/5 years ago and then we started researching and reading literature and we saw that it is actually working in different places and there are different experiences. (Interview TNZ6)
>
> Actually the idea of PBF comes from partners and the MOH. (Interview TNZ7)

The history of PBF is similarly complex and embedded in political shifts in the health sector in Zambia. The overall picture from Zambia is that while the idea of implementing health system reform based on results and performance is not new – PBF had been previously used by the now defunct Central Board of Health in the mid-1990s as a tool of health system reform – current incarnations of PBF are new and are being driven by the World Bank and the Global Fund. There is some evidence of local government officials (and also mission facilities) piloting incentive systems in relation to maternal health services in the eastern province district of Katete (see MoH, 2011). There, the system in place had a considerable focus on local 'demand' however, involving, for example, the provision of mama kits to new mothers at delivery centres (napkins, pins, soap, Vaseline), gifts to traditional birth attendants for each set of five pregnant women delivering at the health facility, and food provided at antenatal clients. There was also a 'supply' side payment of US$285 for the best performing health centre (MoH, 2011). However, there is little information about the history of this initial initiative. The subsequent development of the World Bank-funded pilot appears to have been influenced by the new availability of external funding through the HRITF. When asked for more detail, a senior government official involved in the World Bank-financed Zambia pilot admitted that such projects come about when someone in Washington has an idea and offers the country money to implement it – countries want the financial resources and so they choose to do the project:

> You know, you know how the World Bank is. Someone comes up with a concept paper, pushes it on the country. They push. They ask if you want the money, you want the money, so you do the project. (Interview ZAM3)

This view was supported by another government official who had an association with the Zambian pilot:

> I think it was, you know when they propose that there is this project, so then we applied for that project as a government. So there was, we were informed by the World Bank there is the project, would you be interested? So we said yes we would and we applied for it and we started from there. (Interview ZAM1)

Government officials associated with PBF were keen to assert the Zambian ownership of the project; however, they were also resistant to any general questions about how the programme was designed and how indicators were identified. Only those officials no longer working with the World Bank or the Ministry of Health were open to sharing information. In these cases, they clearly indicated that the project was led and designed by the World Bank and that the enthusiasm for the project was on account of the money being made available to the ministry.

In South Africa, interviewees similarly suggested that PBF had been around for an extended period of time (it was claimed that the province of Limpopo used PBF schemes in the late 1990s), predating the Rwanda pilots and the interventions of the Global Fund in 2002. All respondents in South Africa understood the current approach to PBF as a representation of an externally driven form of financial management founded on a two-level rationale. One, that PBF was a way for funders to limit corruption by increasing the level of accountability by recipients. Two, that PBF was a mechanism for funders to 'get their money's worth', or as one respondent suggested, 'to get more bang for their buck' (Interview

SA1). What is interesting in the South Africa case is that in contrast to Tanzania and Zambia the application of PBF takes place within a tense relationship between the government, the Global Fund, and the World Bank. The South African government cancelled negotiations on its only World Bank PBF project due to an inability to reach mutually acceptable terms and a general belief by the then-Minister of Health that the World Bank loan would undermine national self-reliance. In the case of the Global Fund, there is a history of the national government being unable to secure grants due to the ineffectiveness of its CCM as operated by SANAC. Consequently, it was a widely held view that the South African government was traditionally an ineffective partner with global institutions, local NGOs, and provinces. This was seen as limiting the agency of South Africa in key global policy debates and as hampering the use of international funds as a 'bridging mechanism' for health system strengthening. As one respondent claimed:

> Things are changing under the new leadership. Since 2009 there is a better sense of co-operation between the local and the global – within SANAC, the DoH and from the new Minister of Health. Prior to that many global funders were shut out from working with the South African government because the minister disliked the West, particularly the US. (Interview SA2)

As a result, in the past most Global Fund money was awarded to provincial governments and NGOs (Western Cape and KwaZulu-Natal – Lovelife and SoulCity) effectively sidestepping the national government and undermining the formation of a more unified national health system. This is because, due to the Global Fund's framework document, which allows PRs to be non-governmental or non-national bodies, CCMs outside of SANAC were organised, creating new avenues for health reform and resulting in increased tension and competition between domestic political players. In this regard, PBF mechanisms of the Global Fund had effectively become a tool for political and health brinkmanship where provinces like the Western Cape could outscore national performance on health, making their claims for national autonomy more salient. Thus, the origins and promotion of PBF in South Africa are complex and represent a mixture of Global Fund allowing for opportunities (both economic and political) for health initiatives that were attractive for a variety of reasons. It also created a form of internal competition for funding, which generated a level of compliance with

DOI: 10.1057/9781137500151.0007

Global Fund priorities and its preferred reporting methods more likely. Nevertheless, South African actors also used funding for focused gains (both health related and politically) and were therefore in some sense 'gaming' the system in relation to broader political and social issues in South Africa, not all of which have resulted in a strengthened national health system.

The origins of PBF in South Africa, Tanzania, and Zambia tell us four things about performance and participation in relation to health system reform in Africa. The first is that performance-related health system reform has existed in Africa for over 20 years and African governments have clear ideas of what PBF should look like in their countries. However, the evidence also suggests that the ability for African governments to independently set the agenda and shape PBF depends to a great extent on how rich and reliant on external aid the country is. This is because in the case of both Tanzania and Zambia, respondents indicated a greater willingness to accept PBF schemes from donors due to the infusion of needed cash this would bring, whereas many South African respondents held a much more sceptical view of externally driven PBF schemes, often suggesting their greater ability for self-reliance and the economic capacity to turn down conditional funding. As one South African official claimed, 'we are not fully dependent, we could make do without them [global donors]...this is not the same for a country, say like Lesotho, where they need the Global Fund and as a result have no power to alter the relationship' (Interview SA4). Second, when government ideas of what PBF should look like come up against donor priorities, donors apply a range of brokerage tactics – unintentionally in the case of funding provincial government and NGOs in South Africa or intentionally by developing parallel pilots in the case of Tanzania – to implement preferred models of PBF. Third, in Tanzania and Zambia current incarnations of PBF are donor-driven and the momentum, scale, and application of this model of health system reform are driven by multilateral and bilateral donors; this is not the same in South Africa where there is more effective government resistance to such external pressure. Fourth, the notion of PBF as evidence of south-to-south learning is challenged by countries that question the success and origins thesis offered by global funders of PBF models in Rwanda and by facilitation through donor-driven study tours.

DOI: 10.1057/9781137500151.0007

Consultants and brokers

Earlier in the chapter it was argued that PBF as a tool of health reform in South Africa, Tanzania, and Zambia is not based on a straightforward relationship between principals and agents. The PBF pilots in Zambia and Tanzania involve a complex combination of donors and government agencies that make up the principal and, in Global Fund PBF, there are multiple and overlapping principal–agent relationships. Principal–agent relationships are further complicated by the use of brokerage mechanisms, which, as the origins of PBF suggest, donors enact in order to try to produce the 'right kind' of PBF reform. The use of consultants is key here, and indeed PBF design, implementation, and evaluation often depend on such individuals, who act as brokers between principals and agents. The use of brokers is an intrinsic part of getting governments to implement the scale, form, and targets that donors prefer, and is thus a key means by which donors seek to consolidate their control and status within PBF aid relationships.

Brokers can be international accountants that assess whether key indicators or targets have been met (as in the case of the Global Fund's system of PBF): NGOs or private companies that work with external funders at the national level to manage smaller NGOs or a region of health centres; national research teams involving universities or research institutes; or, in some instances, UN agencies such as the UNAIDS. These third parties have been used throughout the PBF pilot projects in Zambia and Tanzania (helping with project management, training, implementation, and also independent verification of reported results), and also feature in many stages of the Global Fund's PBF process (including proposal development, indicator selection and target setting, and also verification of results). Third parties in many ways have the most direct impact on how the financial relationships embedded within PBF schemes operate in practice as they often decide or arbitrate on what constitutes performance. For example, PricewaterhouseCoopers (PWC) as the Tanzanian LFA has a core role in adjudicating and interpreting indicators for the Global Fund:

> It's a bit of a challenge and again it will depend on which indicator you are talking about. Some indicators are also the information from the head office, other indicators are from information from local government authorities and that is always a challenge, if there is a mismatch between what you see and what is reported and what is seen from local government authorities. It is a challenge. And I think the countries are working with us are seeing that,

DOI: 10.1057/9781137500151.0007

but that is a challenge that has been there, since, if you look at the previous reports, you will see that some of the indicators are really targets, simply because some of the regions have them in their report this time or some will be there, probably the reporting period is not relating to the period under review. (Interview TNZ8)

Brokerage has long been a central function of UNAIDS, which has often positioned itself as an 'honest broker' and intermediary in the governance of HIV/AIDS (Harman, 2010); however, UNAIDS has extended its role considerably with regard to working with governments on securing Global Fund money: (1) It works with national governments to write the grant proposal – this is usually technical support and data provision (if requested); (2) The Global Fund TRP will ask UNAIDS how feasible the grant is and filter this into the overall decision for grant approval; and (3) UNAIDS may be contacted to give evidence regarding the effectiveness of target reach. Hence, UNAIDS brokers through all three of these PBF stages and has executed this role in relation to our case study countries in the past. When asked if this creates conflicts of interest, UNAIDS interviewees said no; insisting that UNAIDS acts objectively and that as long as this is perceived as such by all sides, then UNAIDS' reputation will be enhanced and policy effectiveness increased (Interview SA3).

In the case of South Africa, it was widely suggested that professional health consultants had too much influence on how PBF targets were selected and on how to best meet those targets in relation to the Global Fund. As a senior official in the Ministry of Health lamented, 'these consultants come in and say this worked in Rwanda or Nigeria, yet they cannot always explain why this is suitable for South Africa' (Interview SA4). The problem, according to several interviewees, is that the consultants are usually extremely instrumental in the final decision, and although this can capture elements of partnership when exercised in concert with government, it can also be a way for government officials and donors to abdicate responsibility, or for consultants to promote certain policy choices where there is weak internal organisation. In addition, once a Global Fund grant was in place, it was also suggested that the mechanisms used by the Global Fund to monitor and track performance required the continued use of external consultants, which reinforced PBF logics and such a brokerage role. As one interviewee explained, 'this reliance is due to the fact that Global Fund requirements and paperwork are too complex and constraining and that some recipients find it is easier to hire consultants than do it yourself' (Interview SA5). Here, brokers

DOI: 10.1057/9781137500151.0007

have to some extent become indispensable because they are 'expert' in translating Global Fund requirements to country recipients and also in translating local performance back to the Global Fund in Geneva. Yet in some interviews, the accounting agents used by the Global Fund (in the South African case KPMG and PWC in Zambia and Tanzania) were criticised for the way in which this role was executed, given that it regulated the timing of activities within the health sector. In South Africa, the LFA was, for example, held to be 'useless' and blamed for delays in funding rollouts because KPMG had to 'run everything through its US office' (Interview SA5).

International consultants and accountancy firms are an increasingly common feature of global health and international development. In all sectors of international public policy, financial accounting has replaced accountability. PBF is in many respects the natural extension of this process: payment occurs only by return on investment. The use of consultants in a brokerage role is important here for three reasons. The first is that brokers as mediators fracture any straightforward relationship between the principal and agent that PBF reforms are supposed to engender: brokers face in two directions (cf. Bierschenk et al., 2002) – mediating between donors/governments/health centres/health workers at different times – and therefore effectively occupy the role of both principal and agent at once. This in many respects undermines the perceived accountability function of such PBF as there is confusion as to who is the principal and agent, and thus who is holding who to account. Second, brokers are self-serving. Their role is written into contracts and the accountancy base on which PBF rests makes them indispensable to the reform process. Third, brokers can shape the pace, timing, and means through which African actors participate in shaping PBF outcomes, design, and implementation. They do this in multifarious ways, by, for example, delivering in-country training to ensure the right kind of understanding of PBF, by performing a gatekeeper role with regard to who has access to principal donors, and by ensuring the right kind of PBF targets are set by agents. Brokers are thus intrinsic to the reproduction of the right kind of knowledge on PBF. At the same time, brokers reduce the direct space for participation and partnership between principals and agents because they add an extra layer of engagement. Combined, these factors undermine the quality of participation in PBF processes and, perversely, may reduce accountability among both principals and agents in PBF.

Target setting, gaming, and the right kind of PBF

Questions as to the role of brokers and the ownership of PBF programmes in South Africa, Tanzania, and Zambia are most acutely visible by looking at who sets, negotiates, and approves the targets and indicators for performance and what happens when expected results are not met. Donors are keen to stress that target or indicator setting is an iterative process that takes place between the principal and the agent. However, our research indicates that while these iterative practices do take place there is evidence to suggest the outcomes of such processes can be distorted by pilot schemes and by donors changing the performance goalposts after an agreement is signed.

Pilot schemes

In Zambia and Tanzania there was evidence to suggest that pilot projects have been used as a means of brokering agreement between the government and donors, so that donor-preferred targets and indicators are set. It was widely suggested in Zambia that the World Bank had effectively steered many of the types of targets used within the PBF pilot programme. As one Zambian official claimed, 'the World Bank had a number of key interventions that they wanted to see implemented and they were very firm in their demands' (Interview GEN3). Representatives from the Ministry of Health at the national level were involved in negotiating which targets and indicators would be used; however, those at the facility and district level that would be implementing the project were not fully engaged, particularly at the formative stage of the initiative. In some cases, this appeared to have shaped the way the scheme was received by agents at this more local level. As one staff member in a clinic commented:

> When PBF was starting, it was a challenge because to some of the staff it seemed as if they were just testing the people on their capability to do the work, but for now this is when we have seen the results. (Interview ZAM4)

The situation was similar in Tanzania. Here, the pilot project was developed not principally by the MoHSW using HMIS indicators but by the Ifakara Health Institute in partnership with international donors. As one respondent described the process:

DOI: 10.1057/9781137500151.0007

P4P, the original plans and the original design and all of that had no involvement from CHAI whatsoever, it was designed by Ifakara Health Institute, it was you know it came out of the agreement between Tanzania and Norway partnership initiative and CHAI was nowhere on the map there. I think part of the reason maybe from Norway's perspective that they did approve or seek out CHAI was the work CHAI had done on HMIS strengthening in Mtwara, in Lindi, and so because also pay for performance was intended to augment and support and use the existing HMIS and also validate HMIS data to the point that they could be paid on, you can't bring on a partner that doesn't know HMIS to do P4P the way that it is designed. You know you could do a totally different design that didn't require that level of expertise, but since there was that level of investment in HMIS, because CHAI had existing experience and was, I should say, the most successful so far as getting the results that were wanted using the existing system for HMIS, it was seen as a natural extension that P4P could leverage that experience. (Interview TNZ9)

South Africa is different compared to Zambia and Tanzania in that evidence showed that health officials at every level were able to push back on the demands of donor principals during initial negotiations about external funding and PBF agreements, targets, and indicators. The reasoning for this ability to push back was linked to South Africa having a stronger economy and a less externally reliant health system. In terms of target setting within South African Global Fund grants, there was a general consensus that the CCMs (both national and provincial) were able to set their own targets. As a result, for the most part, South African CCM members and health officials believed that there was a good sense of national ownership and that the setting of targets was done mostly through internally driven mechanisms. Yet, there was a general feeling from South African recipients that external funders involved in the Global Fund process did attempt to informally steer deliberations towards certain target areas or target outcomes in line with particular donor interests. Several interviewees also suggested that the Global Fund itself (i.e., in Geneva) would make strong hints in relation to the type of outputs that would be 'more likely to be approved by the TRP' and to firmly suggest what sorts of target deliveries would be deemed successful. In its most cynical form, one national health representative who was present in Geneva went so far as to suggest 'that PBF is not a partnership or representative of national ownership' (Interview GEN7). This interviewee suggested that PBF targets and mechanisms might be fairly negotiated in some cases, but that in South Africa, and indeed

DOI: 10.1057/9781137500151.0007

elsewhere, funders often dictated the terms of agreement, changed policy at the last second, scratched out line items from the grant, and 'expect[ed] the applicant to do as they are told' (Interview GEN7).

However, this cynical interpretation of the effectiveness of the Fund's pressured 'steering' was not fully born out from the majority of interviews. In terms of how targets were set, targets mostly corresponded to the NSP. According to one interviewee (Interview SA12), who was a consultant for the Ministry and Department of Health and working on implementing the NSP, new grant targets reflected about 90% South African self-targets and 10% international targets, which are dominated by the Millennium Development Goals (MDGs) or UNAIDS 3 Zero programme (although South Africa added a fourth zero) (Interview SA12). National targets were largely being set by national figures generated from the newly formed Department of Monitoring and Evaluation (although there was widespread agreement that this data was often incomplete) or through other external sources (e.g., UNAIDS) and consultations. Furthermore, discussions about grant targets with external funders have been deliberated through the development partners' forum in collaboration with the South African CCM. As a result of these forums, the general consensus was that 'there is now a good marriage between the national and global, and the global targets are always discussed and taken into account' (Interview SA6). What this indicates is that although the Fund will attempt to steer and shoehorn national targets into their overall PBF vision, there was room in South Africa to manipulate and set targets themselves. That said, the question remained as to how much the targets were 'self-selected' because it was understood that they would meet with TRP approval or whether these targets were solely based on South African priorities (there is also the possibility that the Fund's priorities matched South African concerns and therefore consensus was naturally delivered). Where firmer 'conditionalities' were set was in the form of monitoring and reporting requirements, in which pushback was deemed difficult if not impossible.

Targets, indicators, and data quality

The most obvious source of indicators for each PBF project would be HMIS data, given that this is a core data set in each country. However, in some cases existing HMIS data was not seen to be sufficient to support PBF projects and thus additional indicators from outside the country were introduced in order to create the 'right kind' of PBF project. The P4P project in Tanzania was accompanied right from the start by a programme of work to amend the HMIS, so as to ensure that it would support the P4P process. The dismissal of HMIS data points to a recurring theme in all case studies: the general belief that PBF can only be successful with proper monitoring and evaluation systems in place and that current systems were often held to be ineffective in capturing the necessary data required to successfully set and evaluate targets.

Many interviewees suggested that poor pre-existing monitoring and evaluation systems within each of the case study countries caused several interrelated problems with PBF design (and also with monitoring and evaluation). First, it was widely held that without reliable health estimates it is difficult to know the scope of the problem from which targets should be set and measured against at the design stage. Second, without reliable information regarding existing health delivery, it was seen as almost impossible to know specifically what gaps in service delivery existed and what new targets would work best to complement existing infrastructure. Third, without knowledge of existing systems and their effectiveness it was difficult for different actors to participate in the design of PBF targets and indicators, as it was hard to estimate reliably what targets are achievable and what targets are unrealistic. Fourth, without effective monitoring systems it was impossible to adequately measure and report on performance, and thus evaluate the success of delivery on targets. Fifth, there was no clear way of differentiating between externally funded programmes and internal programmes in order to measure from which activities target results were generated or realised.

Concerns about data quality, reporting, and measurement and attribution issues were not just limited to the poorer countries of Zambia and Tanzania. In the case of South Africa, nearly all respondents claimed that the health sector did not have proper systems in place and further suggested that not all service providers had complementary systems, which fundamentally hampered data coherency. In relation to setting targets, a person in charge of national statistics claimed:

> The most problematic element, however, is that there is not enough good data collection mechanisms in which to confidently set targets to. The quality of data is very poor and almost non-existent and the main problem is related to denominator issues. No one seems to know what denominator to use and it is a matter of guesstimating. There will always be better ways to

guesstimate ... but if the information is limited, your guess will be [limited] too. (Interview SA7)

In relation to attribution issues, a number of interviewees in South Africa suggested that the Global Fund would sometimes claim that particular health results were due to their funding, yet their funding was only part of the picture: wider activities undertaken by the national government or other health initiatives were likely to have contributed in different ways. As an advisor for UNAIDS remarked:

> It is hard to tell what targets are being reached by Global Fund support and what targets are related to national or other organisational activities. The Global Fund has traditionally funded 'activities' and not necessarily 'impact' in terms of overall health system strengthening. As a result, pinpointing what affects the Global Fund has is difficult to know and it is increasingly difficult to link system-wide improvements to particular Global Fund activities. (Interview SA3)

This view was supported by a senior member of SANAC in South Africa who claimed:

> What the Global Fund claims on their website in terms of impact is false. They cannot make distinctions between what their money is actually doing and what the system as a whole is doing. For example, in South Africa, the Global Fund is roughly responsible for 1–5% of ARV needs, yet they claim higher numbers based on national statistics, which reflect the system as a whole. As a result, the national results skew Global Fund results ... this is a massive problem with the Global Fund and one that the Global Fund knows about but is unwilling to face. (Interview SA4)

When asked why the Global Fund would not wish to tackle this issue, this interviewee claimed that it 'would not go down well with external funders and it would effectively hurt the Global Fund in terms of donor support' (Interview SA4). In other words, the Global Fund was protecting its own interests here and was, in the process, effectively protecting its system of PBF from wider critique.

The problem of effective data and measurement under PBF becomes all the more problematic and indeed baffling when looking at how indicators and targets work in practice. On the one hand, implementing agents in all countries reported that there was often 'zero flexibility when it comes to meeting targets' (Interview SA8) – either in relation to the Global Fund's system of PBF or the pilot PBF projects in Zambia and Tanzania. To illustrate the difficulty of altering target indicators, one interviewee from USAID gave an example of a Global Fund grant in Indonesia where a target needed to be changed because imperfect information was incorporated into the grant proposal and agreement. This information was later discovered to be inaccurate. To change the target midway through the grant, both the WHO and UNAIDS had to formally sign a declaration stating that the information was wrong due to no fault of the Indonesian government and that new evidence was more reliable. As the interviewee suggested, 'this took a very long time and effected the roll out of the programme' (Interview SA3). With regard to the Global Fund and the World Bank respectively, other respondents noted:

> There is no flexibility in regards to external circumstances. This is particular[ly] problematic in cases of extreme currency fluctuations where funds can be reduced by 20% within a quick period of time leaving principle recipients underfunded, yet responsible to deliver the same targets agreed to prior to the economy tanking. (Interview SA3)

> I feel that the assessment tools are not good, for example on the partograph, you may be questioned once you just forget to put a mark and for that they score you a zero out of 65 points. Basically, I feel that this is a discouragement because there is a need to be advising me than scoring me zero. (Interview ZAM4)

On the other hand, there is evidence to suggest that donors consolidate their position as principals within PBF relationships by introducing new targets and indicators once contracts have been formalised and signed. It was reported, for example, that the World Bank and the Global Fund often changed or amended these at the last minute or during the implementation phase. Alterations could take the form of line items being struck from a grant document just before implementation or could take the form of requests to add certain provisions to official documentation as PBF projects were scaling up. In South Africa, a former PR argued that the Global Fund often 'changed the goal posts and as a result lost the trust of many partners' (Interview SA9). In addition, several private sector actors suggested that 'the private sector dislikes uncertainty, especially when investment is involved' and that the Global Fund's continued last minute alterations were threatening future involvement in Global Fund projects in South Africa (Interview SA9). The problem with such alterations was that they were seen as unidirectional: donors could make requests as conditions changed, but recipients were not able to amend expected targets easily as new information emerged or conditions changed on the ground. As a result, a number of interviewees questioned

DOI: 10.1057/9781137500151.0007

the quality of relationships within PBF, suggesting that 'although we are participating in discussions, the effectiveness of those discussions is often not equally distributed' (Interview SA5).

Gaming

As Chapter 2 highlighted, gaming is a core problem of PBF (Ireland et al., 2011; Kalk, 2011). Gaming can be defined as 'reactive subversion such as 'hitting the target and missing the point' or reducing performance where targets do not apply' (Bevan and Hood, 2006: 521). Defined as such, gaming was found to be evident in all countries, yet was particularly raised as an issue in relation to the process of negotiating PBF agreements associated with the Global Fund in South Africa. In particular, there was reported to be a tendency for government and/or civil society implementing agents to over- or underinflate PBF targets, so as to either please their constituents or help secure a good Global Fund performance ranking. It was reported, for example, that civil society organisations had a tendency to underinflate their targets in order to try and assure output success. As one CEO of a South African NGO suggested, the possibility of future funding was dictated by how well targets were achieved: since NGOs often relied on this funding for their survival there was a tendency to be conservative with targets to make sure that they scored highly and continued to receive funding. The implication of this is that the output capacity of the NGO could actually be higher, yet remains underutilised to maintain performance and apparent success. In relation to government targets, it was suggested by some interviewees that government officials tended to seek to overinflate targets in order to make it look like they 'take health seriously and are doing something about it' (SA10).

It was generally accepted that gaming also occurred during the implementation of PBF schemes, in the sense that the need to meet projected targets brought with it trade-offs in terms of whether efforts should be directed towards reaching specific health targets at the expense of wider quality of care. In South Africa, nearly all respondents suggested that PBF incentivised short-term outputs over long-term outcomes during implementation of health service work, although the scope of the problem was not clear and there was little official evidence to corroborate this general belief. A range of examples of trade-offs were recounted in interviews (which supports the work of a number of other studies also highlighting this issue such as Ireland et al., 2011 and Langenbrunner and Liu, 2005). One example was reported in Tanzania: a clinic claimed 100% target satisfaction for prenatal visits and services rendered, but under closer inspection, it was found that visits were not only shortened but also did not deliver the full range of expected care services to patients (Interview TNZ3; Ifakara, 2013). Another example relates to a Global Fund-related ARV programme for children in South Africa, in which a target of 100% access to ARVs was set. Although the target was reached, it was reported by one interviewee that the quality of care was poor and the level of professional staffing was 'not of a high standard' (Interview SA7). The interviewee further indicated that 'many corners were cut' and that, over time, there was a risk that these poor practices would become the norm, making it harder to alter in the future.

Measures can of course be put in place to try to deal with this particular form of gaming. In Zambia, for example, non-incentivised indicators are also routinely monitored at facility level within the World Bank pilot: if these fall below 80% of the expected trend, corrective measures may be set and/or a performance contract nullified (see Ministry of Health, 2011). The implications of this process are not, however, currently clear. Moreover, there are questions as to whether it would be possible and sustainable to nullify the performance contracts of facilities if PBF is scaled up and rolled out in future.

Interestingly, accusations of trade-offs by interviewees in South Africa tended to be made in relation to other government departments or service NGOs. Indeed, not one interviewee in South Africa claimed that trade-offs took place within their own organisation, preferring instead to point fingers elsewhere. One explanation for a lack of evidence concerning trade-offs and an unwillingness to admit outputs at the expense of overall quality of care and health outcomes is that PBF systematises a culture of omitting information to make sure funding continues without undue investigation. That said, several NGOs in South Africa suggested that trade-offs are less likely to occur within the NGO sector, since their need to maintain reputation for future funding acted as a 'check and balance' on NGO behaviour (Interview SA10). As one NGO director explained:

> [Organisation X] doesn't see a reduction of quality in relation to reaching outputs, but I see potential for this to occur elsewhere. I think those who have established records are less likely to reduce quality, since poor quality would leak out and destroy its reputation and any further funding. (Interview SA1)

DOI: 10.1057/9781137500151.0007

Proponents of PBF suggest that it is an intervention in the health sector that will produce better data and better systems of monitoring and evaluation as it is an accountability tool at heart. However, as the above issues suggest PBF is in many ways complicating the data problem by introducing indicators and targets that are different to that which is captured in HMIS, introducing multiple pilots that overlap, replicating and running parallel to existing initiatives within the health sector, and then introducing additional indicators while remaining rigid to what is expected of agents. Underpinning these problems is the dubious legality and consequences of what happens when a state does not meet the indicators and targets set/agreed by an international donor. Most donor–recipient agreements include arbitration clauses; however, there is some confusion as to which law these clauses pertain to. The assumption is that such contracts fall under South African/Tanzanian/Zambian law; however, this may depend on the country and funder. As one interviewee in Zambia explained:

> Most of the arbitration clauses start by saying that if there is a difference we will try and amicably resolve, which is the situation I told you about before. If it fails we will try the arbitration law of the implementing country so in this case we follow the arbitration act here in Zambia. And the arbitration act says you appoint an arbitrator who is mutually acceptable to both parties... There are times when the donor has insisted that the applicable law, there is a clause on the applicable law, so the applicable law will be like the US but we have refused. We have refused in most cases in almost all cases to say that is not correct because we want the applicable law to be in the implementing country, where the implementation of the project takes place. In this case the project is taking place in Zambia and the applicable law should be the law in Zambia. And that clause is in all our contracts. (Interview ZAM2)

The idea that the default law is not that of the country in which a programme is implemented suggests a legal asymmetry to PBF relationships that has not been fully explored in existing research on the topic. One issue here, which was evident in the case of South Africa, is that a lack of clear arbitration procedures seems to be exacerbating tensions between those involved in the Global Fund's system of PBF; and this may distort or negatively affect PBF as a mechanism of health reform. For example, the Ecumenical Foundation of South Africa (EFSA) was audited in 2011 through a diagnostic report conducted by the Global Fund Inspector General and with the LFA brought in for support. The EFSA's grant was suspended due to the report, yet the report was subsequently found to be incorrect and the LFA did not verify the Inspector General's account. The arbitration process involved one year of costly legal battles and resulted in no funds for seven months. As was claimed during interviews, there was no independent verification of the report, there was little communication during the investigation, and, following the legal proceedings, no feedback in the evaluation process. Such an incident and the confusion over the legal basis for much of the PBF agreements show how the legal basis of African agency can come into question through this mode of funding health system reform.

Another cumbersome and fragmenting fad

Part of the objective of PBF is to reduce confusion and cut through bureaucracy within health systems, yet these reform outcomes have been challenged in material presented above. The application of any new method of practice within a health system inevitably has teething problems and can initially be quite cumbersome. However, the complexity of different sources for indicators and targets, a process of gaming the setting of targets, and the introduction of new indicators and targets after an agreement has been made has exacerbated these issues, generating confusion within the health systems of Zambia, Tanzania, and South Africa at best and creating a burden at worst.

PBF schemes introduced under the Global Fund were criticised in particular in all case study countries for being burdensome, inflexible, and not always fit for purpose. In the South African case, there was a general sense that the Global Fund may no longer be worth the administrative hassle. Monitoring regulations were seen to be overly draconian and, at times, hindered existing local systems that had to incorporate the external reporting mechanisms. The level of frustration at cumbersome reporting conditionalities was sometimes expressed in terms of 'economic colonisation' and a belief that the conditions on performance monitoring were overly restrictive; limited rollout of HIV/AIDS, TB, and malaria programmes; consumed administrative resources; and acted on the 'assumption that fraud and corruption must exist' (Interview SA5). Respondents in South Africa expressed external pressure to change existing governance systems to meet Global Fund demands (sometimes reasonably or unreasonably). According to different high-level officials:

DOI: 10.1057/9781137500151.0007

The Global Fund has become overly cumbersome in terms of paperwork and the Global Fund continues to change the conditional regulations, but not always with sufficient warning. (Interview SA8)

The Global Fund gave one week notice that we were to implement a new system and they were unable to schedule the needed technical assistance until after the forms were due. (Interview SA11)

The Global Fund changes frameworks without notice or consultation. This causes confusion at the national level. This also forces us [UNAIDS] to provide additional assistance to help governments/NGOs understand the changes and this can cause shortages in UNAIDS capacity to help. (Interview SA3)

In all three case studies there was a particular concern that the vertical nature of PBF more generally could compound the already existing level of fragmentation within the health systems, given the large volumes of funding that PBF schemes tend to attract (e.g., the Zambian project focusing on maternal and child health is nearly US$17 million). As one African health representative in Geneva suggested, 'PBF creates "health silos" that are well funded, but not necessarily integrated into the overall health system' (Interview GEN2). For some, the extra initiative of finance that PBF brought was feeding into a parallel health system in Zambia and Tanzania where the health systems are weak. In Zambia, the Ministry of Health was split in 2012, resulting in the setting up of a new Ministry of Community Development and Mother and Child Health – it is currently unclear how this wider shift will impact on the PBF scheme in terms of its current implementation and impact, and on the way the project interfaces within the overall health system.

Distortion in a country such as South Africa is perhaps less noticeable due to the more advanced level of the health system and the organisation of workers in the system. However, the belief that PBF could lead to increased fragmentation was still apparent in all interviews within South Africa. In particular, there was a widespread belief that the past failures of SANAC to capture Global Fund grants had led to provinces and NGOs designing and implementing their own Global Fund programmes without national co-ordination. As a result, having multiple PRs operating independent Global Fund grants within South Africa was contributing to perceived inequalities in health service distribution among provinces and contributing to areas of neglect in terms of overall HIV/AIDS, TB, and malaria services available.

DOI: 10.1057/9781137500151.0007

Reproducing positive bias

The concerns health officials have about PBF could in many ways be expected given that no reform to a health system is easy. As indicated earlier in this book, the health systems of Zambia and Tanzania are reliant on external aid (at 40.2% and 27.8%, respectively; WHO World Health Statistics, 2014) so it is also perhaps expected that external actors will want to have some decision over where their money goes, even if they are committed to principles such as country ownership. However, one of the main sticking points to the implementation of PBF that gives additional weight to the concerns that have been reported above is the seemingly positive bias that has been adopted by influential proponents of PBF.

The first concern around the positive bias is the extent to which PBF has been fully debated as the most appropriate and effective tool of health reform in Africa. The rationale for PBF holding a favoured position in global health policy is not always clear. Respondents from the WHO stressed that there was a general lack of debate about PBF and that it was often assumed that it was the most effective mechanism. The belief that PBF works was widely held despite an inability by many respondents to cite concrete evidence. At best, respondents were able to point to a small number of particular cases where PBF had been seen to be effective (usually Rwanda and Burundi), but the direct evidence for such claims was often admitted to be based more on 'everyday conversations and not from any report or evidence' (Interview GEN6). As one African WHO country representative remarked:

> These sorts of [PBF] programmes are very popular and their effectiveness is often assumed. I don't think there is a great deal of argument taking place about the risks of these types of funding mechanisms... on the whole donors and consultants are in favour of target-driven financing and they have successfully entrenched this as the primary mode of operation. (Interview GEN3)

There was some level of agreement that most external funders are open to discussion regarding best evidence and, therefore, that if evidence showed that PBF was not working or was only useful in certain sectors, then it could be replaced. As one interviewee indicated, 'there is a debate taking place and it is a matter of knowing what works and doesn't work. People are swayed by the evidence, the problem is having reliable evidence' (Interview GEN2). There are clearly spaces for African actors to engage in the process of interpreting evidence and, indeed, many African

DOI: 10.1057/9781137500151.0007

actors are employees of leading agencies such as the World Bank, WHO, and Global Fund. The process of using evidence and formulating new policies relied on informal linkages and networks within and between these agencies and African actors situated 'outside' national institutions. As one World Bank staff member indicated:

> I mean take our health strategy for example. That was put together over a period of many months that had, yes, there were formal consultations around that, but it was just as much shaped by multiple interactions that happen at the country level, the global level etc, conversations that help to evolve the team's thinking. And then you have iterative feedback both with outside partners and staff within the Bank so it goes to a process where you have a document that is reviewed by the senior management of the Bank and approved and sent to the Board for endorsement but that is after much informal and iterative processes. (Interview WAS3)

While external funders who were interviewed were certainly keen to indicate that more evidence was needed about PBF, the collection of more evidence seemed to be presented as a simple precursor to the future scaling up and further rolling out of this approach, rather than part of a process through which PBF will be critically reflected upon and a possible decision made not to proceed with the approach. The positive stance towards PBF appears to be institutionally embedded within the World Bank, USAID, CHAI, and the Global Fund. Similar to what we saw in the HRITF blogs in Chapter 2, any critique from these agencies tends to be about how PBF can be improved upon, rather than a debate about alternative mechanisms of health system reform and financing. The effect of this is the reproduction of the positivity and the silencing of alternatives.

The positive approach to PBF represents a governance bias that is reproduced by the World Bank, USAID, CHAI, and Global Fund through financing of pilot projects, commitment to investment in health system reform, the financing of study tours to Rwanda, and the production and use of the 'right kind' of knowledge that stresses the benefits rather than the challenges of PBF. Reflecting on the positive stance towards PBF, a key purpose of the HRITF is to build the evidence base on health sector PBF initiatives, or rather to build the evidence base *for* scaling up PBF. As one interviewee remarked:

> Part of what the Bank is trying to do as part of the trust fund, [is] to build the evidence for this...I think this multi-donor Trust Fund is a really important

institutional mechanism, a really important learning opportunity for the world. (Interview WAS1)

As Chapter 2 demonstrated, this 'learning opportunity for the world' presents a skewed version of PBF that celebrates the positive impact and potential of PBF while obscuring the challenges and negative aspects of such a reform tool. Hence the HRITF reproduces what the Bank sees as the right kind of knowledge on health system reform that does not challenge or explore alternatives to PBF but advises countries how to adopt the strategy and improve on it. Government officials within Tanzania and Zambia appeared to be complicit in reproducing a positive stance towards PBF given the significant volumes of funding that PBF programmes bring. As one Tanzanian health official explained:

> We found evidence of non-PBF success, yet the Ministry did not want to hear this because it would affect future funding from the World Bank for national rollout. In the government report on P4P, World Bank methodology was used and never questioned. Even though there is evidence to suggest problems with P4P, the government is acting counter to this evidence. (Interview TNZ4)

In many respects PBF is sold as a panacea for problems of tracing where the money goes, stimulating progress, and rooting out incidents of government bottlenecks and corrupt practices. This is a powerful 'sell' as these issues cause common frustrations among civil society organisations and international donors. It also allows sectors of health ministries to present themselves as dynamic in invoking alternative forms of project implementation. However, in many ways, this powerful sell is underpinned by a thin evidence base that goes largely unquestioned by those health systems that desperately need more funding.

Conclusion

This chapter has shown that far from being an African-led panacea to problems of bureaucracy and results in delivering on MNCH, HIV/AIDS, malaria, and TB, PBF is in many ways seen by African agents as another donor-driven fad that is cumbersome and bureaucratic. The principal-agent model that PBF rests on is undermined by the complicated ways in which PBF projects are set up and by an extra layer of consultants and agencies that act as brokers. Country ownership and African demand for PBF is questioned by the way in which targets and indicators are set

DOI: 10.1057/9781137500151.0007

and verified. The implementation of PBF as a tool of health reform in Africa exemplifies how knowledge in global health is reproduced to meet donor concerns and interests and shapes policy outcomes to meet such ends, and is thus far from the idealised model of 'evidence-based policy'. Donors would suggest that these interests are mutually constituted with national governments and civil society actors through engaged partnership on health system reform. However, as the next chapter shows, ideas of participation vary and are asymmetrically weighted towards the interest of maintaining a positive bias towards PBF strategies and those elites within health systems that are set to benefit from it.

DOI: 10.1057/9781137500151.0007

4

The Politics of Participation in Health Reform

Abstract: *This chapter examines how multi-sectoral and multi-level stakeholders have participated in the formation of performance-based funding (PBF) design and implementation at the global and national levels in South Africa, Tanzania, and Zambia. The chapter looks at what is meant by participation and what we know about its role in health system reform, and formal and informal mechanisms of participation at multiple levels of governance. In so doing, it demonstrates the dominance of informal mechanisms that undermine meaningful participation as they privilege elites, lock out other stakeholders from the participatory process, and maintain a positive bias towards PBF with little meaningful engagement. The chapter also explores the problems of participation fatigue and the culture of per diems and paying for participation.*

Keywords: elites; formal and informal participation; participation fatigue; paying for participation; per diem

Barnes Amy, Garrett Wallace Brown and Sophie Harman. *Global Politics of Health Reform in Africa: Performance, Participation, and Policy.* Basingstoke: Palgrave Macmillan, 2015. DOI: 10.1057/9781137500151.0008.

DOI: 10.1057/9781137500151.0008

The evidence and argument presented in Chapter 3 suggests that perform-ance-based funding (PBF) as a tool of health system reform in Africa has been introduced and designed by international donors and reproduced through financing to African countries. More developed states are able to push back on such reforms where they see them as bureaucratic and counterproductive to their agenda, as in the case of South Africa: less developed states such as Tanzania and Zambia find themselves in a bind between attempts to evoke ownership in keeping with the Paris Declaration on aid effectiveness and curtailing to donor preferences to access much-needed funds to support concerns such as maternal and child health. This picture would suggest that African actors have limited agency in donor negotiations if they want to secure funding. However, this overlooks the complexity of participation and the relationships that exist between international donors and African actors. This chapter argues that there is evidence of formal and informal participation in the design and implementation of PBF as a tool of health system reform in Africa. African actors *are* engaged in the formation of PBF as a means of health system reform; however, participation is often limited to specific elites working in the health system whose continued pay is dependent on alignment to the positive bias of PBF. These elites engage in a skewed principal–agent relationship with donors through whom they gain mate-rially or politically as individuals. This is particularly the case in Zambia.

The aim of this chapter is to understand how participation works in the design and implementation of PBF programmes and to show how participation is skewed towards the reproduction of a positive bias towards PBF as a tool of health system reform. To pursue this aim the chapter first outlines what we mean by participation and how the concept is used in global health policy. Second, the chapter then consid-ers how participation works at the global level of engagement in global health policy hubs such as Washington, DC (World Bank, the United States Agency for International Development (USAID) headquarters) and Geneva (the Joint United Nations Programme on AIDS (UNAIDS), WHO, Global Fund headquarters). Third, the chapter explores how participation works at the national level and the informal and formal spaces available for engagement between donors, government, civil society, and the private sector. Fourth, the chapter reflects on the issue of per diems and the wider politics of paying for participation to which PBF contributes. The chapter then draws its main findings together in conclusion.

DOI: 10.1057/9781137500151.0008

Understanding participation

As outlined in Chapter 1, participation refers to the ability of different agents or stakeholders to engage with and shape health policy at the global, regional, national, and local, for example, district/ward level. It is a key operating principle to how global health policy is meant to be formed and implemented. The World Bank, WHO, UNAIDS, the United Nations Development Programme (UNDP), United Nations Population Fund (UNFPA), and the Global Fund all sign up to some form of participation as a key component of how they deliver on global health priorities. All bilateral donors that are signatories to the Paris Declaration on aid effectiveness are similarly required to adopt a participatory approach to the development and application of global health initiatives. The rationale for participation is threefold. The first is a reaction to the top-down conditional-based aid lending that typified the relationship between global health donors and recipients in the 1980s and early 1990s. Instead of donors telling states what to do with aid money the idea is for states and donors to participate in the design and implementation processes in a way that produces mutually agreed priorities, strategies, and policy. The second explanation for a growth in participation is the need to include all aspects of society, not just the government, in global health policy as health is provided by a range of actors: practitioners, non-governmental organisations (NGOs), faith-based organisations, the private sector, and advocacy groups. The rationale here is that any policy that is designed purely by the state or the international community may not take into account the concerns of those that implement the policy, hence all relevant stakeholders representative of specific sectors of society should participate in the policy process. The third rationale for participation is to have a plurality of interests and ideas in the policy process to prevent the dominance of a particular approach or form of thinking about global health problems. Health is embedded in socio-economic inequalities and thus delivering health policies requires multi-sectoral approaches to health problems that takes these factors into account when designing policy and strategy. There is agreement among commentators that national and sub-national ownership of health programmes and political commitment to them is vital to the design, implementation, and sustainability of schemes (Atun and Kazatchkine, 2009; Brenzel et al., 2009; Eichler, 2006; Eijkenaar et al., 2013; Levine and Oomman, 2009; Low-Beer et al., 2007; Magrath and Nichter, 2012; Oxman and Fretheim,

DOI: 10.1057/9781137500151.0008

2009; Toonen et al., 2009). As such, participation has normative value, as we have seen, as well as practical relevance. For example, Low-Beer et al. (2007) argue that civil society is an efficient implementer of PBF as 83% of the programmes implemented by civil society in their study performed strongly. Furthermore, increased community involvement improves overall health system governance as service providers become more accountable to the communities they serve and ensure that schemes are scaled up to reach less accessible groups (Atun and Kazatchkine, 2009). The rationale for participation thus seems straightforward and its adoption as a working principle of global health governance shows promise for participatory forms of decision-making. However, there is also evidence in the literature of concern over the extent to which donors and international organisations engage in meaningful participation and the consequences of participation in practice (Harman, 2010).

Recent scholarship has emphasised the importance of understanding not only the temporal dimensions to participation but also the importance of understanding the spaces and places within which participation can occur (Cornwall and Coelho, 2006), and particularly the ways in which different global actors, such as the WHO, World Bank, and Global Fund provide such opportunities. The Global Fund is often heralded as a 'better' exemplar of participatory global governance (Brugha, 2004). Its Board is multi-sectoral in that it is made up of both aid-giving and aid-recipient countries and is inclusive of civil society and the private sector. The Board has been praised for its uniqueness, substantial developing-country representation (Sridhar and Batniji, 2008), and as a positive step towards representation in global health governance (Buse and Harmer, 2007). In addition, the Global Fund's main in-country operating structures – the Country Co-ordination Mechanisms (CCMs) – are often cited as examples of best participatory practice and points of access to health governance for local stakeholders. As indicated in Chapter 3, CCMs are made up of a combination of government agencies, civil society actors, and private sector stakeholders and are supposed to oversee Global Fund operations, manage and disburse grants to principal and sub-recipients of Global Fund money, and liaise with the Global Fund in Geneva. Feachem and Sabot (2006) argue that the Global Fund model has empowered civil society in many countries, Zambia among them, by providing points of access to decision-making processes – in 2006, 40% of CCM members came from civil society. Kelly and Birdsall (2008) point to the restructuring of the CCM in Tanzania into a

DOI: 10.1057/9781137500151.0008

National Coordinating Mechanism that incorporated the US President's Emergency Plan for AIDS Relief (PEPFAR) and World Bank resources as a success in broadening participation and partnership.

However, there is much evidence to suggest that there is a politics to such participation within both the CCMs and the Board. Brown (2009; 2010) identified voting cleavages in the Global Fund's Board, with civil society and recipient representatives facing voting coalitions that were often pre-organised by donor representatives prior to Board meetings. There is also a loophole in civil society involvement in CCMs in that it is recommended rather than required (Brown, 2009). Contrary to investing in community and civil society projects, the Kelly and Birdsall (2008) study shows that at the time of their research, nearly 80% of Global Fund funding went to the Tanzanian Ministry of Finance and found that civil society organisations in Tanzania feel that their roles have been prescribed by external actors as a direct result of funding modalities. Other more recent studies in Zambia, India, and the Soviet Union have highlighted competitive power struggles and tensions that shape engagement in Global Fund processes more broadly, and draw attention to the ways in which Global Fund structures might entrench existing hierarchies within the health system and provide only token-istic opportunities for the participation of smaller civil society organi-sations (Barnes, 2011; Kapilashrami and McPake, 2013; Harmer et al., 2012).

The problem of skewed participation is echoed in studies on the World Bank. Harman (2010) has shown how participation in World Bank-supported HIV/AIDS programmes in Africa has been limited to the 'usual suspects', meaning those civil society organisations familiar to the government and international donors. World Bank participatory structures are set up so that it is difficult for those affected by the Bank's programmes to directly engage with the institution: all participation has to go through national and local government bodies. Hence, participation in World Bank-funded projects is structured in a way that minimises the Bank's involvement and stresses the role of state agencies as the key part-ners for engagement. Participation takes place in-country where World Bank projects are implemented: not in the World Bank headquarters in Washington, a key hub of policy knowledge and design. Participation is limited by multi-levels of engagement that leads to confusion as to who is able to participate at which level and who is responsible for policy decisions and implementation, and ostracises those actors who are not

DOI: 10.1057/9781137500151.0008

familiar with the system of governance implemented for HIV/AIDS programmes (Harman, 2010).

Issues with the participatory processes in the Global Fund and World Bank have led to calls for greater alignment with the Paris Declaration when it comes to providing aid and funding for health systems, especially in relation to country ownership and local capacity building (Biesma et al., 2009). This call is echoed by Sridhar and Batniji (2008), who highlight that other aid sectors have been more effective than the health sector at complying with the Paris Declaration and focusing on country ownership. They argue that political economy analysis of donor institutions would support understanding of their decision-making processes, and further highlight the need for 'the development of country ownership, particularly planning and priority setting' (Sridhar and Batniji, 2008: 1189).

What we therefore know about participation in global health policy is that it is accepted as a practice of global health governance and something that is to be strived for. We also know that global institutions have formal participatory processes in place that can both limit and enhance participation; the evidence as to how effective and meaningful this participation is appears to be mixed. However, these studies tell us less about how multiple levels of participation intersect or how the different stakeholders involved in participation interact. The line of inquiry tends to be international donor + other, be it the state, civil society, or the private sector. These categories in many respects are taken as homogeneous groups; this in part may be just intellectual shorthand, but it importantly overlooks the myriad of relationships that take place within civil society, donor institutions, the private sector, and governments. For example, governments are not unitary actors; an official from the PBF team of a Ministry of Health team may participate in decision-making on PBF outcomes in a more direct manner than an official from the maternal health section of a ministry. A World Bank representative working in-country may have different ideas of participation than an official working in headquarters in Washington. It is therefore important to recognise difference within and between stakeholders participating in policy processes associated with PBF.

In addition, there is little clarity about the normative assumptions about what meaningful participation should look like, or empirical data about how those who are involved understand how it operates in practice: it is something that the global health community prioritises but there is very little understanding of what good participation is and means. This chapter addresses these lacunae by looking at participation at multiple levels of engagement, and by recognising heterogeneity across the different stakeholders involved in participatory processes of PBF design and implementation. In so doing we can begin to think about what existing limitations there are to meaningful participation as well as reveal the politics at every level of participatory engagement in the development of PBF as a tool of health system reform in Africa.

Global formal and informal spaces for participation

Evidence from national case studies and global-level interviews illustrates that there are many formal and informal mechanisms for participation between government, external funders, international agencies, private agencies, and civil society organisations at different levels of health system governance and in relation to PBF more specifically. As will become clear, however, the issue here is not whether participation occurs, but how it proceeds, who is involved, and thus the overall quality of participation involving African actors and the extent to which participation can be considered as a partnership.

Global spaces for participation refer here to the global policy health hubs of Geneva and Washington, DC. Some authors argue Atlanta and Seattle also constitute global health hubs because of the headquarters of the US Centers for Disease Control and Prevention and the Bill and Melinda Gates Foundation, respectively; however, Geneva and Washington are home to clusters of intergovernmental organisations, civil society organisations, and philanthropic foundations that have headquarters or representatives in-country. Geneva is the home of the UN health agencies (apart from UNDP and UN Women in New York) and the Global Fund. Washington is home to the World Bank, USAID, and representative offices of multiple health agencies. It is at these global health hubs that policy and strategy are debated and agreed on, budgets and allocations are set, stakeholders are convened, and knowledge is produced. Even though policy-making takes place and can be subverted at multiple levels of governance it is the global health hubs of Geneva and Washington where overarching policy ideas, themes, budgets, and decisions are made. Hence participation at the global level, informal interaction with and between leading development agencies is the central mechanism to participate in, influence and shift the global health policy agenda, including the development of new strategic policy ideas such as the use of PBF.

The World Bank has significantly increased its engagement with civil society organisations, faith-based organisations, and the private sector at the global level, since reforms as to how the Bank operates were implemented in the late 1990s. However, formal spaces for such groups to participate in the operations of the Health, Nutrition and Population section of the Bank in which PBF falls under are relatively closed. The main formal space for civil society and private sector actors is in pre-determined sections of the Bank such as the global Civil Society Team. With regard to formal spaces for participation and partnership within the Bank, the following quote sums up a common response:

> So when you say who are the partners on a day to day basis it depends on where you are working. There is no list that you check off, these are the partners... we do discuss and debate a lot within the Bank, maybe even more than academia because we are at that sweet interface between knowledge and practice it's a lot in the Bank and each debate is over whether there is a formal approach, you say 'this is the amount of partnership' – I doubt that, I would be very worried if everybody at the same time, all the time, I think something would be wrong there.... So I'm not sure that it is reasonable to expect an institution in which everybody would agree that 2.1 doses of partnership is the way to go, 7.5 doses of partnership is the way to go, it is not physics. (Interview WAS3)

The Global Fund in Geneva similarly only makes formal space for participation of those actors who sit on the Board. In both cases, these institutions preferred to engage formally with in-country partners at the national level through mechanisms associated with a particular project and delegations from headquarters going on field visits. Less value was placed on engagement in Washington or Geneva by these institutions as being intergovernmental in nature. African actors sat on different decision-making panels in the wider institution, and it was seen as vital that policy issues affecting a specific country should be discussed in that country through technical working groups. Global Fund personnel suggested that there are good communication flows between the TRP, the Global Fund Secretariat, and the applicants. Although it is often the case that the TRP requests further clarifying information – or in drastic cases, suggests reworking the application – the Global Fund interviewees insisted that all communication is in written form and records are kept

DOI: 10.1057/9781137500151.0008

for legal reasons. As one Global Fund respondent stated, 'the substance of the grant is "nationally owned" and the CCMs are not influenced by what they think the Global Fund wants to hear' (Interview GEN1).

Despite a lack of formal channels of communication at the headquarters level those working in the World Bank were keen to stress their openness to informal means of communication. The general notion across different sectors of the World Bank and Global Fund was in-country partners, that is, government partners could contact project managers and coordinators at any point via email, telephone, or in person if necessary (Interview WAS2). There was no apparent systematic closing off of participation of these actors: there was just no formal mechanism for inclusion either. The onus here was on the institutions reaching out to stakeholders when in-country and if the stakeholders want to engage at the global level it was up to them to do so.

Some global-level interviewees suggested that informal networking is particularly important in relation to PBF given the few formal channels for discussions on PBF to take place (Interview GEN3). External funding modalities and performance targets tend to be negotiated at the national level and on a bilateral basis – between those receiving and those providing the funding. This bilateral process does not allow for much diplomacy in discussions in formal global health policy spaces or for much regional involvement. Opportunities do exist for African delegates to the UN or African WHO representatives to discuss informally such an issue. For example, one interviewee indicated the usefulness of informal conversations for altering perceptions regarding the types of interventions that should be pursued via PBF. As one interviewee commented:

> Geneva is a small place and we all know each other. We often chat about what's working and what's not, what needs more attention and what's getting too much. These chats filter into WHO policy and these policies affect the operations of the Global Fund and World Bank. (Interview GEN3)

However, in many respects the WHO operates outside the push for PBF. The WHO is not involved in the models designed by the World Bank or the Global Fund. The Global Fund was deliberately not housed within the WHO as it was seen as a barrier to the Fund's purpose and vision (Brown, 2010). As a result, the WHO itself has seen a shrinking participatory role in how global health is financed. As a senior African representative at the WHO suggested:

There is not much scope for discussing funding modalities.... I mean it does come up, but more in terms of the system needing targeted aid, and more of it. We largely discuss policy in terms of priorities, strategy and practice, not on the details of aid delivery. (Interview GEN6)

The formal spaces that exist to discuss global health policy centre on broader health policy areas, themes, or issues (e.g., maternal health, child health, under-nutrition) rather than specific funding modalities (Interview GEN2; Interview GEN6). This situation was not seen to be desirable at the global level, particularly since aid funding provided through PBF tends to shape the wider process for governing funding and budgets within African health systems. As a result, a number of interviewees expressed some level of frustration that PBF was not being, what they called, 'properly' or 'fully debated' in WHO (Interview GEN2; Interview GEN6).

The case of the WHO is interesting as it is one of the key institutions where African governments have a formal seat at the table and have the potential to work together in African voting blocs to increase the impact of their participation in the institution. It is also the only global health institution that is made up of regional sections. However, at present, it is felt that there was not much coordination in pursuing an African agenda at the WHO in terms of policy direction, including on PBF. As one interviewee indicated, African diplomats 'come to the table too late' and have to operate within 'an agenda that is already set'. The key 'is for us to better set the agenda so as to get our needs better addressed' (Interview GEN3). Regional platforms were seen as a potential space for participation but these were underused in global decision-making forums such as the WHO (Interview GEN6). It was generally felt that the WHO lacks 'punch' and is not effective in taking a lead in global policy. As one interviewee stated, 'the G8 can set policy faster and more effectively than the WHO' (Interview GEN6). Hence, even if African governments and the African region of the WHO were to open up participatory processes of discussion around PBF policy in the WHO at headquarters level this would have little impact as the debate and financing of PBF is not happening within the institution and for some it has an increasingly redundant role in global health policy and finance.

Global spaces for participation in Geneva and Washington suggest the following about how we can understand participatory processes in the design and implementation of PBF as a tool for health reform in Africa. Informality does not engender a relaxed and engaged relationship

DOI: 10.1057/9781137500151.0008

between the Bank, Fund, and the stakeholders they collaborate with on PBF, but limits the space for participation as stakeholders have to justify why they want to engage at the global level before they are able to fully participate. A preference for informal engagement also presupposes that key stakeholders know how to engage and who to engage with and that they are able to navigate through complex institutions such as the Fund and Bank. Informal participation risks excluding those actors with an interest in PBF who may not know the language, networks, and individuals or have the resources they need to engage to get access to decision-making. In this sense a preference for informal participation is a deliberate tool of those working in the Bank and Fund to seem approachable – all the while selecting those key people they want to engage with and to do so on their terms. Emphasising national engagement appears to be an attempt to circumvent the Bank and Fund from any agency or responsibility at the global level for what happens in-country. This is fundamentally problematic when considering the evidence in Chapter 3 that shows PBF was designed in these global health hubs. Formal engagement with a strategy for inclusiveness that focuses specifically on PBF would enhance the responsibility, transparency, and accountability of the Bank and Fund's role in health reform in Africa and would fully resource a range of actors to participate in a clear manner. Informal participation at the global level leads to fuzzy engagement and policy-making that remains skewed towards the positive bias of the international donors outlined in Chapter 3. The response of the Fund and Bank to this argument will no doubt be that participation in global health policy-making happens at the national level through such mechanisms as the CCM. Yet, as Chapter 3 showed, this is questionable and as the next section demonstrates fraught with the same difficulties associated with informality.

National formal and informal spaces for participation

Participation in policy design, formation, and implementation of PBF is all said to take place in-country at the national and sub-regional levels. This is perhaps obvious given African governments use their legitimate power derived from a relationship with South African, Tanzanian, and Zambian citizens to take the lead in shaping the content of health system

DOI: 10.1057/9781137500151.0008

reform within their sovereign borders. Hence it would seem logical that decisions on African health system reform take place in African countries by African governments. This is a logic stressed by international donors such as the World Bank and Global Fund and underpins the central components of the Paris Declaration. However, in practice the case of decision-making is less straightforward as the decisions and policies taken by African governments are often subsidised or steered by international donors who have their own policy preferences that can complicate the policy-making and implementation process. It is this complication that makes participation tricky, particularly with regard to how to create participation in situations in which there is a difficult balance between ensuring African sovereignty and allowing international donor input so as to generate effective partnership. As this section shows, this balance is challenged not only by the practical workings of formal spaces that exist for participation and the prominence of informal partnerships at every level of health governance but also by the use of participation as a tick-box activity, as a type of policy procrastination, and as a means of supplementing public sector incomes.

At the national level, a range of formal and informal spaces exist for African actors to participate in the design and implementation of various PBF programmes. Technical working groups, annual review meetings, subcommittees, and formal networks all exist within the formal system of health governance in the three case study countries. These report and feed back to each other and provide institutionalised spaces for African actors – government ministers, civil servants, civil society organisations, development partners, and the private sector – to engage with one another and with local aid agencies. Development partner forums in each of the three countries provide a coordinating space for partnership among international funders that exist separately, but this is supposed to feed into government decision-making processes. In addition, these meetings are designed to avoid programme overlap and to make sure there is PBF target coherency between externally funded projects and internal national strategy plans.

In South Africa, the South African National AIDS Council (SANAC) works alongside the development partners' forum to invite NGOs, service providers, and civil society organisations to be involved with all aspects of grant design for the Global Fund. This not only helps to legitimate SANAC as the main coordinating CCM but also in many ways allows PBF to retain its favoured position in relation to external

DOI: 10.1057/9781137500151.0008

funding. Almost all interviewees confirmed that the level of partnership at the national level in relation to the Global Fund had increased since SANAC was reformed after 2009 and that this signalled an important step towards greater partnership between internal and external entities. As one respondent remarked:

> SANAC is more multisectoral with five NGOs [all former Global Fund principle recipients] on the panel who are involved in the joint grant. Partners can bring their own grant ideas and deliberation between partners is very good and open. I think the relationship between NGOs and SANAC has improved, although we remain cautious about NGO's moving from service providers to technical assistants, since no one knows what this means yet. (Interview SA1)

In Zambia and Tanzania, many of the members of the CCM are also formal members of the technical working groups, review meetings, and sub-committees that were referred to above. This crossover is seen as a way to ensure some level of joint engagement and coordination across the health sector. Proposal development processes in both countries are also designed to be open and collaborative, and are advertised as such in local media.

In relation to the pay-for-performance (P4P) project in Tanzania, the Ministry of Health and Social Welfare (MoHSW) has endorsed the P4P approach through the Health Sector Strategic Plan. This means that elements of P4P are approached and discussed within the day-to-day and institutionalised spaces that exist within the health system as part of the country's sector-wide approach (or SWAp). At the same time, new project management bodies have also been set up to oversee the delivery of P4P. For example, advisory and steering committees have been established to offer strategic direction and a management team involving professional PBF consultants oversees operations and meets regularly. National and regional verification committees verify district and facility reports, respectively (Borghi et al., 2013). In Zambia, formal mechanisms follow a similar referral process between the Ministry of Health, the Provincial Medical Office, and the District PBF Steering Committee (MoH, 2011). Such formal mechanisms of engagement build on previous sector-wide or SWAp approaches to health governance. Hence, participation in PBF is based on pre-existing in-country models developed in collaboration with international partners and civil society over the last 20 years.

The entrenched formal models of participation show a commitment, openness, and will towards a collaborative policy process. Interviewees in all case study countries deemed important the inclusion of a wide range of actors and there were many examples of positive progress to broaden the basis for participation in health. Invariably, however, participation at the national level is shaped by many factors, including local histories of engagement, pre-relationships on the ground, and political events that occur outside the health system as the discussion below highlights. The existence of formal institutional structures and the presence of different actors may signify participation; however, these alone do not suggest effective participation or that all actors play an active role within these structures. There tends to be a distinction between who talks and who listens in formal spaces for participation. In some cases, a divide was found to exist between external funders and the government. For example, even though some external funding agencies are acutely aware of the need to let the government lead and participate as partners, in Tanzania and Zambia government officials often appeared to prefer to co-lead or let external funders 'do the talking' at times. This was evident in the observation of annual programme reviews in Tanzania in which external funders were keen for government to chair and lead break-out discussions and plenary debates. However, in practice, Tanzanian government representatives would wait to see how the development partners would articulate a specific issue before speaking: the government chair would first thank the external funders for supporting operations and then pause to let the development partners fill the silence and steer the discussion. The development partners would then eventually try to focus the discussion on the problems encountered in the health system, time would run out, and little would move forward.

In relation to the operation of Global Fund processes in South Africa, almost all interviewees in the country argued for more input and evaluation from independent civil society organisations that could validate claims and let officials know how things are going on the ground. This is because nearly all interviewees argued that strong CSOs can increase pressure for transparency and can 'hold public officials to account in ways that formal PBF mechanisms cannot do alone' (Interview SA12). The response to civil society involvement in Tanzania and Zambia was generally positive, with most interviewees from government and international donors giving a standard response: that civil society enhanced transparency and enabled multi-sectoral approaches to health. However, interviews with civil society actors highlighted a level of frustration at how participation was increasingly captured by large international NGOs and/or umbrella group representation. Some organisations wanted to

DOI: 10.1057/9781137500151.0008

have direct representation on structures like the CCM and felt they were being managed by either an international NGO, who was often acting as the principal recipient for Global Fund monies, or the umbrella representative. They were therefore concerned that their views were not being heard and that there was a formal block between them and the funders that supported their projects.

The formal spaces for participatory dialogues with civil society organisations in the World Bank PBF programmes were slightly less clear and appeared to be more *ad hoc*. Civil society organisations can feed into PBF programmes through the existing formal structures within the health system outlined above but there was less formal inclusion in PBF-specific meetings. For example, in Tanzania the P4P Advisory Committee is made up of the MoHSW, Regional Medical Officers, Ifakara Health Institute – a think tank, GIZ – a technical global health and development consultancy, USAID, and the Clinton Health Access Initiative (CHAI). Additional observers are welcome, and indeed do attend these meetings; however, this is much more informal and tends to have low representation of civil society, principally national civil society groups. In Zambia, formal engagement with civil society organisations in the meetings and discussions on PBF is again minimal, with occasional representation from key national faith-based organisations such as the Churches Health Association of Zambia (CHAZ) that have a long history of working in the Zambian health system (see also Ministry of Health, 2011).

In principle, communities are supposed to participate in the Zambian World Bank PBF pilot, in terms of monitoring and evaluation and the verification of patient satisfaction performance data, for example. In reality, however, community participation appears to have been variable and shaped by pre-existing histories of local participation and the pre-existing quality of the interface between facilities and local communities (Interview ZAM5). Zambia has for some time built community participation into the health system, in the form of neighbourhood health committees. However, these were mostly supported by user fees. When user fees were removed at the primary care level with the removal of the Central Board of Health, the level of community participation within the health system was affected, with formal structures for participation ceasing to function in some areas. The level of oversight and involvement exerted by communities in the PBF pilot is therefore shaped by this history and the pre-existing structures that are available for participation.

DOI: 10.1057/9781137500151.0008

While there has been anticipation that PBF will bring enhanced community participation, some local-level interviewees seemed to narrowly conceive participation as working with communities to encourage women to deliver within facilities, rather than their involvement and oversight of the performance judgement process (Interview ZAM5).

There appears to be a similar situation in Tanzania. While community participation is built into P4P project documents, with a role in the verification process, there appears to be an absence of mechanisms and resources to ensure community involvement in verification processes and some evidence of variability across the different districts involved in the P4P process (Ifakara, 2013). Participatory processes for the implementation of the World Bank's style of PBF are thus more between international donors, civil society organisations involved in the implementation of the projects, consultants, and those members of government responsible for the project.

One explanation for why there is low direct involvement of a wide range of civil society organisations in formal PBF meetings associated with the World Bank, USAID, and CHAI is that they are not invited or seen to be relevant. Another explanation is that meetings with the wider health sector, if functioning well, should suffice. The other explanation is that they are invited but do not attend. The latter is a growing problem with participation in health system reform in Tanzania and Zambia, where many respondents stressed how they thought participation was a good thing but it was becoming too onerous because there was too much of it.

Faith-based groups such as the CHAZ in Zambia and Christian Social Services Commission (CSSC) in Tanzania are seen to be effective partners by international donors and government and, as a result, are invited to multiple different meetings on a range of issues. This clearly puts a demand on key individuals' time – especially those who are seen as trouble-shooters that get things done – and can produce participation fatigue. A common result is that actors say yes to many meetings, even when they clash, and then decide which is the most important to attend on the day. This becomes evident in meetings, such as those observed in Tanzania, in which there are clear discrepancies between the list of attendees and those who are actually present. This process can cause confusion within the health system, and also resentment or frustration by others who set up or are in attendance at the meeting and contribute to a two-tier level of partnership. PBF adds to this broader situation as it brings with it additional requirements to meet and attend, as suggested above.

DOI: 10.1057/9781137500151.0008

An additional consequence of excessive formal structures for participation is that actors turn to informal means of engagement as a way of circumventing seemingly bureaucratic procedure to get things done. Similar to the global level of participation, a range of informal mechanisms exist for participation at the national level that offers opportunities to shape knowledge and perceptions about the way PBF can and should work, about who is involved in PBF processes nationally and about how targets are set, appraised, implemented, and monitored. Examples of informal opportunities for interaction include lunch meetings, phone calls, text messages, children attending the same schools, and personal friendships. Anyone in the informal loop generally has the mobile phone numbers of a range of important stakeholders and can call upon these people when they need to, without appointment. In all three case studies (and at local through to global levels), informal networks were highly effective in shaping who participates and in making progress on issues.

In relation to the Global Fund's system of PBF in particular, informal connections tend to have a significant effect in determining who is able to access Global Fund funding, with, for example, the selection of recipients of funding shaped by political affiliation or political views. This has been apparent in relation to Global Fund processes in both Zambia and Tanzania and was also perceived to be an issue in South Africa in the past, although mostly pre-2008/2009. For example, in South Africa SANAC was mentioned as in the past having had favourite NGOs that were not always the most efficient or successful, with some NGOs being pushed out because they were not in line with government/minister's political views. These informal processes can thus generate ill feeling, particularly among civil society groups who feel a sense of being locked out of certain networks. Although multi-sectoral participation within SANAC and the South African CCM was widely believed to have improved since 2009, concerns remained about the level of civil society inclusion and inclusion more broadly. As a top official at SANAC stated:

> Civil society groups are not as integrated as they should be...and finding legitimate CSOs is not always easy and there is a great deal of 'political wrangling' between various CSOs looking for access...[rebuilding partnerships] will not happen overnight and that future efforts to bring CSOs into SANAC will be made...at the moment there are more pressing concerns to get the CCM working again and focus needs to remain on this immediate concern. (Interview SA4)

DOI: 10.1057/9781137500151.0008

In sum, there are clear formal structures that provide opportunities for a wide variety of actors to participate in the health system in South Africa, Tanzania, and Zambia. Global Fund structures provide the clearest formal mechanisms of multi-sectoral engagement on issues of PBF financing and reform through recommending that all CCMs attempt to maintain a 40% multi-sectoral threshold beyond government agencies (Global Fund, 2001: Sect. III). The World Bank and CHAI P4P pilots provide less of an opportunity for direct participation with multiple stakeholders and tend to have a government, donor, and consultant focus on participation. All actors seem acutely aware of the need to balance African-led policy with the realities of needing to maintain funding and donor support. The slight exception here is South Africa, which shows a greater ability to pushback due to its limited reliance on external financial support and its history of explicitly viewing many external funders such as the World Bank with a high level of publicly stated suspicion. The replication of formal mechanisms of participation across the three countries is quite telling in how international donors establish their own governance structures such as the development partners group and establish similar policy-making bodies such as the CCMs in different countries. We have seen this before in the case of HIV/AIDS policy in East Africa (Harman, 2010); however, what perhaps sets the new trend apart is how participation is increasingly seen as an onerous burden on the stakeholders. Participation has generated excessive meetings on different health topics, PBF included, which compete for people's time and attention. Exacerbating this tension and competition has been the tendency to pay for participation, which commodifies participation in a way that perverts the normative and practical relevance of enhanced participation.

Per diems and paying for participation

Participation is to a large extent facilitated by and dependent on payment. A number of African delegates in Geneva suggested that the idea of participation came down to the financial relationship of one who pays and one who does not, and thus that partnership is structured on this basis. Payment for participation is the norm in Zambia, common in Tanzania, but less evident in South Africa, perhaps because there are better salaries in the health system and it does not have a legacy of donors

DOI: 10.1057/9781137500151.0008

paying for participation. Per diems are fundamental, as they shape how governmental health officials participate and engage in partnerships with international donors. A per diem is essentially a prospectively determined daily allowance in order to cover approved expenditures (or out-of-pocket expenses) of individuals who are carrying out particular roles (Vian et al., 2012). Per diems can be paid for a variety of participatory processes such as attendance at meetings, attendance at a workshop, or a community visit. The amount of per diem depends on the location of the meeting, workshop, or visit; the issue (e.g., AIDS pays more than TB); sector (e.g., health is seen to pay higher per diems because of the number of actors and initiatives involved in the sector at the moment); and the type of actor (e.g., more if you are a government civil servant than a civil society worker). They tend to be paid by government ministries or by international donors. Some donors do not pay per diems, but most reluctantly do as it is easier to secure participation and thus get things done.

While little has been written about per diems in relation to global health policy processes, a number of studies have highlighted that they are becoming an increasingly common strategy for supplementing the salaries of health workers in African health systems, where salaries tend to be low and/or unreliable (Vian et al., 2012; see also Roenen et al., 1997). A per diem culture presents several consequences for the politics of participation. First, it creates an incentive towards meetings as a means of supplementing an income and thus the number of meetings proliferates. Second, work that does not receive an extra per diem, for example, drafting strategy, filing reports, general administration, becomes secondary to that which is rewarded with money. Third, it can lead to those meetings where a per diem is not paid being ill-attended. Fourth, it creates an artificial market within the public sector where issues popular with the development community (e.g., health or Millennium Development Goal-related priorities) create a pay bubble separate to the banded pay scales of the civil service in these countries. For example, the health systems in Zambia and Tanzania run on public pay scales, grading workers according to their role and level of expertise and/or seniority; additional funds or bonuses risk distorting such scaling and could result in the need to reassess health worker pay across the sector, or result in dissatisfaction across sectors, depending on how the division of labour is organised. Fifth, per diems create animosity between government, civil society, and the public at large who resent government actors 'getting fat' off the government and development aid.

DOI: 10.1057/9781137500151.0008

As was related in a number of interviews and our stakeholder workshop in South Africa, PBF incentive structures feed into the wider problem of a per diem allowances culture in the health sector, particularly in Tanzania and Zambia. PBF adds to the problem of financing dictating health policy priorities because of the money it brings, not only to clinical staff but also staff working in health and associated ministries. New policies such as PBF that are to be implemented inevitably generate extra meetings, workshops, and study tours, all of which are accompanied by payment as per diems or allowances for those who attend. As a result, officials may not attend a different non-PBF meeting for a particular health policy without a per diem, or choose to attend the health initiative with the bigger per diem (e.g., it is further away from their office, therefore the payment is bigger), rather than another meeting that may be of concern.

In many respects, per diems can be seen as an extension of the principal–agent model, in which payment is the incentive, reward, and thus norm for the relationship between a principal and an agent. Per diems fit well with and reflect this wider model, the principal (a government ministry or donor) pays for participation in the delivery of PBF as a form of health system reform, and agents, who are responsible for its delivery, receive payment as a reward for their engagement and participation. The problem here is, however, that this model overlooks the agency and intent of the agents themselves in this process. This is significant because those working in health ministries are complicit within a per diem culture and the idea of incentivising performance because of the extra income it brings, usually to those who are in an elite position. Such complicity is not uncommon and is indeed, in many ways, reflective of studies on neo-patrimonialism in African politics, particularly Bayart's depiction of the 'politics of the belly' in which:

> the apparatus of the State is in itself a slice of the 'national cake' so that any actor worthy of the name tries to get a good mouthful. This partly explains the apparently excessive value attached south of the Sahara to the creation of new administrative structures: offices and public works... These institutions are in themselves providers of riches and wealth. (Bayart, 2012: 90)

The politics of the belly is particularly evident in Zambia where new administrative structures have been created for the management of PBF within both the Ministry of Health and the recently formed Ministry of Community Development and Mother and Child Health; new

DOI: 10.1057/9781137500151.0008

results-based financing steering committees have been created at the district and national levels; new training sessions are arranged to learn about PBF; and new workshops are arranged to discuss targets and indicators. Crucially, per diems tend to be given to ensure attendance at such meetings. There is a clear financial gain for civil servants not only working in the health system but those working in a popular aspect of the health system such as PBF. In interviews, public servants in Zambia would informally praise the health system for being where the highest per diems were, whereas in other sectors, such as education, it was reported to be hard to recruit people as the per diems were lower. One respondent in Zambia informally suggested that civil servants working on PBF drove better cars because they were involved in a new reform tool that was popular with donors.

The result of all of this in Zambia (and to a lesser extent in Tanzania) is a two-tier system of civil servants: those that work in high-profile, well-financed programmes such as PBF, and those that work in everyday health system management that offers less individual material gain. This creates an elite group of actors in the health system that gain financially from the introduction of new health system reforms and have a vested interest in PBF to maintain their material benefits. It is therefore not surprising that those government actors paid to participate in meetings with international donors such as the World Bank are keen to maintain a positive bias towards PBF: it is of individual value to them to keep PBF programmes going as they stand to benefit materially. Here then, per diems are evidence of health system elites using their agency, yet using it to (not) attend and participate meetings in order to gain from international aid and global health policy.

Conclusion

Formal structures for participation in health system reform policy exist at both the global and national levels of decision-making and implementation. However, there are few formal arenas of participation for PBF specifically. PBF relies on formal participation in wider health system negotiations. Participation in PBF design and implementation is marked by its informality that prioritises participation by those actors – particularly elites within the health service or faith-based organisations that often win health delivery contracts – that show a positive bias towards PBF. Such a positive bias is reproduced through

DOI: 10.1057/9781137500151.0008

payment for participation either through the awarding of contracts to particular actors or individual per diems. Payment for participation is exacerbated by a PBF culture that increases individual incentives and monetary reward for health outcomes. The relationship that arises from participation is thus based on a principal–agent model of who pays (usually the donor) and who implements (often the government) with limited reciprocity as to the content of what is being paid for. In other words, participation is a method in which donors can engage governments to fulfil their objectives and use financial incentive as a means of ensuring this. Meaningful engagement that shows evidence of discussion and critique and an adjustment arising from such critique is distinct by its absence in Tanzania and Zambia. This and the foregoing chapters have shown that critique has been evident in South Africa but the consequence of this has been a, at times, tense relationship between the government of South Africa and the Global Fund. Such findings challenge the notion that PBF emerged out of a participatory consensus among key stakeholders in South Africa, Tanzania, and Zambia, and further questions the African nature of health system reform in Africa. The following chapter attempts to draw out and respond to such concerns and offer some final conclusions as to what participation and performance mean for health system reform on the continent.

DOI: 10.1057/9781137500151.0008

5
Conclusion

Abstract: *This chapter outlines the three key findings of the book with regard to the role of African agency; participation and the global health policy elite; and principals, agents, and accountancy in the global health policy market. The chapter then outlines the four problems that the politics of participation and performance demonstrate for health system reform in Africa. Drawing on findings from South Africa, Tanzania, and Zambia, the chapter argues that the theory and practice of participation and performance-based funding remain tenuous, participatory processes of engagement in health system reform are weak, and African agency limited by the robustness of a health system and the nature of existing donor–recipient relations.*

Keywords: African agency; health reform; health policy; market; participation; principal–agent

Barnes Amy, Garrett Wallace Brown and Sophie Harman. *Global Politics of Health Reform in Africa: Performance, Participation, and Policy.* Basingstoke: Palgrave Macmillan, 2015. DOI: 10.1057/9781137500151.0009.

This book has been about participation in the setting and implementation of performance-based funding (PBF) programmes in South Africa, Tanzania, and Zambia as a means of assessing the degree to which African actors set the agenda for health system reform in African countries. PBF was introduced as a new way of financing efforts to reduce maternal and newborn child mortality and reverse the spread of HIV/ AIDS, tuberculosis, and malaria in sub-Saharan Africa. The momentum around PBF led by international donors such as the Global Fund, the United States Agency for International Development (USAID), the Clinton Health Access Initiative (CHAI), NORAD, and the World Bank has led to rhetoric and research that suggests this type of financing model could present a revolution in the reform of health systems more broadly. Indeed, PBF tends to be presented as a panacea to issues of staff morale, procurement, and uptake of clinical services. However, as this book has shown, PBF has a number of flaws, in particular in relation to how the model of principal agency is applied in practice and the confusion and bureaucracy it introduces to health sector reform. It is not a health policy with its origins in Africa or a site of 'south-to-south' learning as was often presented by the World Bank. The application of PBF to health system reform involves the participation of principally elite civil servants and key service-providing civil society organisations working in the health systems of South Africa, Tanzania, and Zambia. This application not only is skewed towards the reproduction of ideas that support a 'success story' model of PBF and the material gain such support brings, but also obscures debate about the ways in which PBF is experienced as a participatory way of reforming African health systems.

This chapter outlines three central findings of the book and the conclusions that can be drawn from them to show that the theory and practice of participation and PBF remain tenuous, that participatory processes of engagement in health system reform are weak, and that African agency is limited by the robustness of a health system and existing donor–recipient relations. The chapter argues that PBF is part of a wider market of global health policy where ideas are bought and sold by donors and recipient states and accountancy is presented as the solution to the politics of reforming health systems. Such a market favours the participation of consultants, often accountants and economists, in the health sector and global policy elites in health ministries and global health institutions. The chapter concludes by outlining four problems

DOI: 10.1057/9781137500151.0009

that the politics of participation and PBF demonstrate for health system reform in Africa.

African agency in the global market of health policy

The first finding of the book is that the introduction of PBF as a tool of health system reform in Africa is framed in the language of south–south learning but that this is subject to capture by international donors, which inhibits rather than enhances the ability of African actors to design and implement African health policy. International donors are keen to assert that the idea for PBF and the mechanism in which it is applied has its origins within sub-Saharan Africa, particularly Rwanda. This is an idea that is reproduced through study tours to the country and donor-funded workshops to promote south–south learning. Nevertheless, many respondents questioned this and the efficacy of the project in Rwanda. In some instances, there was competition over who was doing PBF best, rather than collaboration and learning or grouping together into a regional bloc. Indeed, regional engagement was found to be minimal. Promoting the idea of Rwanda as the originator of the current strand of PBF in health system reform shows a disregard for pre-existing PBF efforts in countries such as Zambia. Instead, previous country-based forms of PBF in the three case study countries have been challenged by a donor-driven commitment to produce the 'right kind' of PBF. This new wave of PBF is ahistorical in that it overlooks pre-existing efforts and subverts what the governments of countries are asking for: either intentionally by developing parallel pilots (as in the case of Tanzania) or unintentionally in the case of funding provincial governments and non-governmental organisations (NGOs) in South Africa in order to implement a preferred model of PBF.

PBF as a tool of health system reform in Africa exemplifies the production and reproduction of knowledge that fits with donor priorities and objectives through commissioning research that aligns with the institutional paradigm, and communicating particular types of research evidence through workshops and globally facing websites. Donors present themselves as passive facilitators of learning in global health policy; however, such learning is limited to specific ideas that are largely unquestioned in official discourse. There is an important distinction between knowledge and evidence that is contestable and refutable, and ideas that can be bought, sold, and reproduced. The World Bank and Global Fund do not produce knowledge that is contestable and proven by challenge outside of their institution, but rather generate ideas that they sell to low- and middle-income countries in the global health market. These ideas triumph in the market of global health policy as they are accompanied by finance and material benefits for those who become enrolled in their development. Such enrolment occurs through the active marketing and selling of ideas as something that governments should want or need, a panacea to their problems. Countries such as Rwanda are a core part of such a marketing strategy and are central to the way in which such ideas are positioned and branded. This market of ideas in global health policy is underpinned by anti-competitive practices however, as global institutions use their leverage and financial subsidies to gain market capture, securing commitment towards specific trends such as PBF. Choice within this market is therefore limited by global health institutions converging around similar ideas and government leverage weakened by donor dependency and their political-economic status.

One key problem with the notion that African actors are sold ideas within the global health policy market and that the Rwandan 'success story' is used as a marketing tool is that it strips African actors of agency, thus reducing them to passive market consumers. Government officials and health workers in Rwanda would no doubt pushback against the idea they are simply a part of a wider donor-driven strategy in the global market of health policy ideas. The Rwanda model has shown some successful gains in maternal and child health and part of this success has been due to the commitment of the health ministry and the central government in implementing and following through on the model. However, Rwanda's size as a small country, consolidated leadership around the Rwandan Patriotic Front (RPF), and the politics of genocide guilt have given it an exceptional form of agency within international development and global health. Genocide guilt gives the government leverage to say no to donors and tell them what they want, and the leadership of Paul Kagame over a small territory is marked by a top-down form of rule that is involved in multiple levels of decision-making (Beswick, 2012), including health. Rwanda is thus not a straightforward success model but an exceptional case.

Countries such as Tanzania and Zambia do not have exceptional or specialised status within global health but are largely donor-dependent countries with limited leverage to say no. Our research shows that the ability for African governments to set the agenda for the reform of African health systems and to pushback on some of the policy preferences articulated outside the country context depends on how well developed a country's health system is. Pushback and saying no was evident in the South African case. Attempts to say no were evident in Tanzania; however, this had little long-lasting effect as PBF was implemented as a pilot rather than a country-wide initiative. The case of Zambia was perhaps the most interesting: those government agents currently working in PBF were keen to stress the Zambian aspect of the design and operation of the project; however, those that worked outside of the PBF team suggested that it was a largely donor-led and donor-designed operation. The less developed a health system, the easier it is to create a PBF programme and set up associated institutional structures, with the risk of creating PBF silos. The more developed a health system and the governance arrangements in place, as is the case in South Africa, the harder it is to develop PBF as a revolutionary mechanism of health system reform.

Governments could of course say no to PBF and opt for an alternative; however, it is difficult to say no to international aid or a specific policy idea when a health system is underfunded and dependent on international donors who are marketing ideas such as PBF. The ability to say no also depends on the wider global health policy market. It is easier to say no to PBF projects attached to HIV/AIDS financing such as the Global Fund because, relative to the rest of the health sector, HIV/AIDS money is readily available and provided for by a range of donors; perhaps not to the same extent as the Global Fund, but there are certainly different finance options and policy choices resting on an albeit narrow range of ideas, not just PBF. Some principal recipients in South Africa have started to resist the Global Fund in this way and they are now proactively seeking alternative forms of support for HIV/AIDS, which do not come with the same requirements as the Fund's PBF.

Choice and the ability to say no for financing options to support maternal health and newborn child health initiatives are much more limited. In countries such as Zambia and Tanzania, where maternal health and child health is poor, financing, particularly for maternal health, has historically been limited. Commitments and strategies towards maternal health and newborn child health have grown since 2003 and the World Bank and CHAI initiatives towards PBF have been part of this (Pitt et al., 2010; Hsu et al., 2012). However, financing options or alternatives to PBF

DOI: 10.1057/9781137500151.0009

remain limited: hence the Zambian and Tanzanian governments have had the choice of adopting PBF reforms as a means of accessing finance for MNCH programmes or continue to underfund the sector and see continued high rates of maternal and newborn child mortality.

The ability of African countries to shape their own health policies may be made difficult by reliance on international aid in a changing global health policy market but that is not to say that there are no opportunities for pushback and change. PBF is also applied to the operations of international donors and the functionality of the brokerage role played by UN agencies and international consultants. Hence, African agents – governments, civil servants, and civil society organisations – can hold such development partners to account for their own activities through formal global performance targets. The extent to which this currently occurs, however, is questionable. African governments could also form allegiances with other countries and civil society organisations as a means to exert influence on donors from outside of the country. Yet regional African alliances on health policy formation are at a minimum and though their potential impact is unknown, working in regional blocs in other areas of global policy such as trade has demonstrated greater African leverage (Lee, 2012).

African agency in health policy reform and choice in the market of global health policy therefore depends on the wealth of a country and existing government finance for the health sector and how well established the health system in-country is. Finance for alternative ideas for low- and middle-income countries is lacking and choice is limited to the current donor preference for PBF. The case of Rwanda shows an interesting example of an African country leading health system reform, but it is not the norm. Current incarnations of PBF as a tool of health system reform in South Africa, Tanzania, and Zambia may have been trialled effectively in Rwanda but they emerged as a result of international donor preferences. How African actors have shaped such preferences varies and appears to be dependent on the wealth, culture, and embedded practices of the health system and the country's political history.

Participation and the global health policy elite

Central to questions as to the degree to which African countries shape African health policies has been participation. This book has argued that

DOI: 10.1057/9781137500151.0009

informal participation presents more meaningful opportunities to engage with PBF than formal participation; however, such spaces are skewed towards the interests of elite African agents. Formal spaces for participation at the global level are restricted and do not specifically correspond to PBF practices and informal spaces are the norm at both global and national levels of engagement. This is particularly problematic when looking at the detail of how specificities of PBF programmes are decided upon. For example, indicators of performance are set at the national level in collaboration with multiple stakeholders; however, donors often come to such collaborations with pre-designed indicators drawn from other countries or global idea centres, rather than in-country data or Health Management Information Systems (HMIS). Participation is not just what happens in formal meetings, but rests on the informality of pre-meeting arrangements and personal and professional relationships. In all three case study countries, there is something of a hierarchy of participation, with access to participation dependent on factors such as status and position (e.g., of individuals in government), relationships to international funders, and awareness of the informal opportunity structures that shape participation.

Excessive forms of formal participation have driven higher incidents of informal participation and the tendency for donors and governments to pay for participation through per diems. While a per diem culture is common to global health policy in Tanzania and Zambia and thus nothing new, the application of PBF is emblematic of this culture and of the way in which it creates a two-tier structure of well-funded health strategies, which can be created within a health service and government system. PBF not only promotes and, to some extent, normalises a culture of reward, but exacerbates the differences between those working with donors in well-funded programmes and those who do not. This difference brings material gain to those who are insiders and an associated material incentive to promote a positive perspective towards PBF. This limits the ability for outsiders to make meaningful contributions to health strategies as they lack the funds to share and implement their ideas.

Again, we see actors within the domestic health setting competing to get their ideas financed in an uncompetitive market of global health policy. For health workers at every level of health system governance there is potentially more to gain from backing a donor-led agenda – bonus pay, per diems, international travel, status within the health system – than there is in emphasising a model of health system reform that does not

DOI: 10.1057/9781137500151.0009

have international finance to back it. Research into alternative models of health system reform in low-income African countries is sidelined in national health policy as justifying the use of public funds in resource-poor settings is difficult and international finance to support research into alternative ideas is lacking. Paying for participation thus contributes to a two-tiered system in African health systems, instead of facilitating dialogue and negotiation, and reduces the plurality of ideas and choice in the wider debate on health system reform in Africa.

In response to the questions posed in Chapter 1, it is clear that the barriers to participation are lack of access to the informal networks and participatory spaces in which decisions are made and, perversely, an excessive amount of formal participation (facilitated in some cases by payment incentives) that devalues the process. Many actors involved in the health systems of South Africa, Tanzania, and Zambia have participated in health forums associated with the World Bank and Global Fund in some indirect way at the national level, through, for example, national strategy discussions or consultations about funding applications. This sort of indirect 'global' participation through national mechanisms was most evident in recent South African development partner forums and within the South African National AIDS Council (SANAC)'s new multisectoral grants collaborations with NGOs and INGOs, where multifarious actors participated in the design of the National Health Strategic Plan, which includes some PBF discussions. In addition, some actors in the policy elite have engaged in regional and global spaces for participation where health financing is discussed as part of larger development aims. However, the quality of this participation is limited because of the number of meetings, workshops, discussion forums, and focus groups that exist in the health sector. Thus, informality largely prevails and meaningful participation in the reform of African health systems is for the most part limited to a global policy elite.

Principals, agents, and accountancy in the global market of health policy

This book has shown that one of the key selling points of PBF that appeals to donors, governments, and civil society alike is that it provides a level of accountability and transparency in the health system, by making clear who is doing what. This is an important part of global health policy as it

DOI: 10.1057/9781137500151.0009

allows the tracking of what is happening, how funding is being spent, and facilitates the identification of potential areas that need further attention. However, as Chapter 3 showed, such accountability and transparency has actually been hampered in practice by way of institutions, such as the Global Fund, setting up a complicated PBF system of principal–agent relationships, changing the goalposts as to what should or should not be measured, and through a confusing use of HMIS and non-HMIS data. In general, respondents felt that far from reducing bureaucracy and creating greater accountability, the application of PBF was cumbersome, bureaucratic, and confusing. The ad hoc nature in which PBF was applied to specific diseases with regard to the Global Fund and the pilot projects for the World Bank and CHAI appear to be leading to confusion as to who is accountable for what. Chapters 3 and 4 show that far from being a revolutionary system of reform, PBF projects can exacerbate bureaucracy rather than reduce it. This is an important critique because it challenges an often given assumption that tools associated with performance and market-based systems of delivery create a wider system of efficiency and accountability.

As Chapter 3 showed, brokers and consultants that facilitate donor–government or principal–agent relations have added an additional layer to the bureaucracy of PBF and to a large degree present an additional barrier to participation. The use of international accountancy and management consultancy firms as interlocutors between global institutions such as the Global Fund and the government or the civil society organisations in which it finances is symptomatic of a wider trend towards accountancy-based governance in global health (Schaferhoff et al., 2014). PBF is inherently an advanced form of monitoring and evaluation that rewards results and good accounting. It is therefore unsurprising that the management of such projects requires accountants rather than public health specialists. The problem here is how judgements are made when certain results or targets are not met and who makes such a judgement. In terms of accountancy and as a representative of PWC in Tanzania indicated, if the recipient does not make the target they do not get the money, irrelevant of whether there is a clear explanation or they hit associated targets. This closes down participation and, on a practical level, can lead to the type of gaming of the system that Chapters 2 and 3 outlined, and a perversion of what is prioritised within a specific health system to meet basic accountancy targets; for example, a doctor may attend to a pregnant woman without complication over treating a man

DOI: 10.1057/9781137500151.0009

presenting with stroke because there is money attached to the pregnant woman. In resource-poor settings, this is an important type of dilemma that medical staff have to face and challenges clinical norms with regard to triage; in attending to the woman they secure extra funds for their health clinic and staff and thus can care for more people as the money keeps coming based on results in this area, but the man presents a more pressing concern and might thus from a clinical position be attended to first. From an accounting perspective, it makes sense for the health professional to attend to the pregnant woman; from a public health perspective the priority would be on the patient with the greatest immediate need. The emphasis of PBF is about gaining rapid results in the much-needed improvement of MNCH, HIV/AIDS, malaria, and tuberculosis; however, the accountancy model on which it rests can lead to the prioritisation of these health concerns over others that do not come with a bonus and this exacerbates distortions within the health system. As a result, concerns were raised in all three case study countries about the negative trade-offs that can exist between reaching PBF outputs and the quality of PBF outcomes. This not only can have a negative effect upon health systems in terms of resource management, be it human or material, but also has potentially long-term negative consequences on overall health system strengthening, since under PBF schemes short-term outputs can be prioritised in order to meet targets, versus prioritising long-term outcomes that may require periods of prolonged scale-up.

The role of accountancy firms as brokers in the implementation of Global Fund projects reflects both a trend towards accountancy-based governance in global health and the problem of implementing principal–agent models. As Chapter 2 showed, principal–agent models underpin the logic of PBF as a tool of health system reform in Africa. The logic of this model would suggest that government acts as the principal and a health centre, hospital, or individual would act as the agent. However, in practice, the principal can be an international donor, an international accountancy firm, the national government, or local government authority and the agent can be the international accountancy firm, the national government, the local government authority, civil society groups, and local health centres, hospitals, and health care workers. Hence, actors often occupy the role of both principal and agent. The only actors that seem resolutely to be agents are the health care workers in health facilities and care and treatment centres; but there are multiple principals. The issue of multiple principals is telling as according to the World Bank,

CHAI, and the Global Fund, the principal should be the government, but as this book has shown, those principals that direct and pay for performance are a combination of international donors, brokers, and civil society organisations, all working within and through government institutions. This complicated and multi-layered system of governance frustrates the straightforward nature of principal–agent theory and suggests that PBF is not being clearly run *by* the government but *through* the government. This has led governments such as South Africa to question PBF initiatives; to Tanzania sidelining PBF programmes into a specific section of the Ministry of Health and Social Welfare; and to Zambia adopting a system of elite principals in a two-tiered health system.

Global politics of health reform in Africa

Participation and PBF have emerged as mechanisms of health system reform in South Africa, Tanzania, and Zambia and as ideas subsidised by international donors in the market of global health policy. Each of the three case study countries has their own ideas and history of PBF; however, the two types of PBF applied by donors such as the World Bank, Global Fund, and CHAI are different in their health topic focus and in the indicators and processes they use to implement PBF. Nevertheless, PBF has gained traction among elites working in the health systems of Tanzania and Zambia through paying for participation and the material gains that reproducing a positive bias can bring. Yet paying for participation, informality, and the excessive demands for formal participation all act as barriers to meaningful participation. The result of which is a two-tiered system of health system governance in Tanzania and Zambia between elites working in well-funded health initiatives and those on the underfunded sidelines of health system reform. As a consequence, it is only those African actors working in the health system that are sympathetic to the agenda of international donors and who engage in the reproduction of positive bias who are fully engaged in shaping health system reform. Contestation and challenge to the positive bias leads to a fragmentation of the relationship, as the case of South Africa showed, and isolation from wider participatory processes and funding schemes in the case of Tanzania and Zambia.

This book has shown several problems with not only PBF and participation in the three case study countries, but four key problems with

DOI: 10.1057/9781137500151.0009

global health policy more broadly. The first is that global health policy can be seen as a market where ideas are bought and sold and where return on investment can take priority over public health concerns. This market affects decision-making, from what international donors decide to invest in to how health professionals prioritise patient care. The market introduces accountants as the arbiters of global health standards. PBF is in many ways the natural product of such a market. Second, participation in global health policy has become to some degree an empty concept: there is seen to be too much of it, and not enough of it in the spaces where it could be more helpful. Informality breeds resentment, maintenance of a positive bias towards particular bodies of evidence, and limits critically constructive engagement in debate. Third, global health policy is elitist; from the elites involved in the production of ideas and policy at the global level to the elites that reproduce those ideas and contribute to the creation of two-tier health systems in countries such as Zambia. Elitism reduces meaningful participation with multiple sectors of government and civil society, limits the space for multiple voices and accountability to the wider population, and is self-reproducing. The result of this is that elites have greater access to the market of global health policy and can frame the debate over African health system reform to maintain their own positions. This privileged elite position could be used to deliver better health outcomes for all, but it could also be used to sideline alternative ideas in the global health policy market. Fourth, there is evidence to suggest that the wealthier the African state and the more well-established its health system the greater the agency of African actors in negotiating African health system reform. As the difference between South Africa and Zambia and Tanzania shows, the more robust the health system and the richer the country, the greater space there is for meaningful discussion and the greater ability to say no to the preferences of international donors.

These four problems are likely to frame the future of global health policy and the future of African health system reform. There is scope for such problems to be addressed or managed in a way that maximises health benefits for all. However, this will depend on elites in government, civil society organisations, and international donors getting used to being told no, and an awareness of the externalities of PBF on the wider political economy of health system reform in these countries. The politics of PBF and participation is not just about international donors telling governments what to do; it is about the reproduction of a positive bias towards particular evidence bases in regard to market-based approaches to health system reform, and the complex multi-level relationships that are required to maintain such a positive bias. This book has challenged the positive bias associated with PBF and has as a result sought to draw attention to what increasingly looks like the emptiness of participation.

DOI: 10.1057/9781137500151.0009

Bibliography

African Union Commission, the United Nations
Economic Commission for Africa, the African
Development Bank (AfDB) and the United Nations
Development Programme (2013). Assessing Progress
in Africa toward the Millennium Development
Goals – MDG Report 2013. http://www.undp.org/
content/dam/undp/library/MDG/english/MDG%20
Regional%20Reports/Africa/MDG%20Report2013_
ENG_Fin_12June.pdf (accessed August 2014).

Atun, R. and Kazatchkine, M. (2009) 'Promoting Country
Ownership and Stewardship of Health Programs: The
Global Fund Experience', *Journal of Acquired Immune
Deficiency Syndrome (JAIDS)* 52 (Supplement 1):
S67–S68.

Bache, I. and Chapman, R. (2008) 'Democracy through
Multilevel Governance? the Implementation of the
Structural Funds in South Yorkshire', *Governance* 21(3):
397–418.

Barnes, A. (2011) *The Politics of the Idea of Partnership: From
Contemporary Aid Policy to Local Health Governance in
Practice in Zambia.* PhD thesis, University of Sheffield.

Barnes, A. and Brown, G. W. (2011) 'The Idea of
Partnership within the Millennium Development Goals:
Context, Instrumentality and the Normative Demands
of Partnership', *Third World Quarterly* 32(1):165–180.

Basinga, P., Gertler, P.J., Binagwaho, A., Soucat, A.L.,
Sturdy, J. and Vermeersch, C.M. (2011) 'Effect on
Maternal and Child Health Services in Rwanda

of Payment to Primary Health-Care Providers for Performance: An Impact Evaluation', *Lancet* 377: 1421–1428.

Bayart, J. F. (2012) *The State in Africa: The Politics of the Belly*, 2nd Edition. Cambridge: Polity Press.

Betsill, M. M. and Bulkeley, H. (2006) 'Cities and the Multilevel Governance of Global Climate Change', *Global Governance* 13: 141–159.

Beswick, D. (2012) 'From Weak State to Savvy International Player? Rwanda's Multi-Level Strategy for Maximising Agency', in W. Brown and S. Harman (eds) *African Agency in International Politics*. London: Routledge, pp. 143–157.

Bevan, G. and Hood, C. (2006) What's Measured Is What Matters: Targets and Gaming in the English Public Health Care System, *Public Administration* 84(3): 517–538.

Bierschenk, T., Chauveau, J. P. and Olivier de Sardan, J. P. (2002) 'Local Development Brokers in Africa: The Rise of a New Social Category.' Department of Anthropology and African Studies Working Papers, Johannes Gutenberg-University. http://www.ifeas.uni-mainz.de/Dateien/Local.pdf (accessed August 2014).

Biesma, R., Harmer, A., Walsch, A., Spicer, N. and Walt, G. (2009) 'The Effects of Global Health Initiatives on Country Health Systems: A Review of the Evidence from HIV/AIDS Control', *Health Policy and Planning* 24: 239–252.

Bohman, J. (2010) 'Democratising the Global Order: From Communicative Freedom to Communicative Power', *Review of International Studies* 36(2): 431–447.

Borghi, J., Mayumana, I., Mashasi, I., Binyaruka, P., Patouillard, E., Njau, I., Maestad, O., Addulla, S. and Mamdani, M. (2013) 'Protocol for the Evaluation of a Pay for Performance Programme in Pwani Region in Tanzania: A Controlled before and after Study', *Implementation Science* 8: 80. doi: 10.1186/1748-5908-8-80.

Bourdieu, P. (1977) *Outline of a Theory of Practice*. Cambridge: Cambridge University Press.

Bourdieu, P. (1986) *The Logic of Practice*. Stanford, CA: Stanford University Press.

Brassett, J. and Smith, W. (2010) 'Deliberation and Global Civil Society: Agency, Arena, Affect', *Review of International Studies* 36(2): 413–430.

Brenzel, L., Bredenkamp, C., Naimoli, J., Batson, A., Skolnik, R. and Measham, A.R. (2009) *Taking Stock: World Bank Experience with Results-Based Financing (RBF) for Health*, World Bank: Health, Nutrition and Population Unit. Available at http://www.rbfhealth.org.

Brown, G. W. (2009) 'Multisectoralism, Participation, and Stakeholder Effectiveness: Increasing the Role of Non-State Actors in the Global Fund to Fight AIDS, Tuberculosis and Malaria', *Global Governance* 15: 169–177.

Brown, G. W. (2010) 'Safeguarding Global Deliberative Governance: The Case of the Global Fund to Fight AIDS, Tuberculosis and Malaria', *Review of International Studies* 36(2): 511–530.

Brown, W. and Harman, S. (2013) *African Agency in International Politics.* Routledge: Abingdon.

Brugha, R. (2004) 'The Global Fund: Managing Great Expectations', *The Lancet* 364: 11–12.

Buse, K. and Harmer, A. M. (2007) 'Seven Habits of Highly Effective Global Public-Private Health Partnerships: Practice and Potential', *Social Science and Medicine* 64: 259–271.

Cockerham, W. (2007) *Medical Sociology*, 10th Edition. Upper Saddle River, NJ: Prentice Hall.

Cornwall, A. and Coelho, V. S. (eds) (2006) *Spaces for Change? the Politics of Citizen Participation in New Democratic Arenas.* London: Zed Books.

De Borman, N. (World Bank) (2014) 'How Can New Technologies Enhance Efficiency and Good Governance of Results-Based Financing?', *RBF Health Blog World* Bank: Washington http://www.rbfhealth.org/blog/how-can-new-technologies-enhance-efficiency-and-good-governance-results-based-financing (accessed October 2014).

Eichler, R. (2006) 'Can "Pay for Performance" Increase Utiliziation by the Poor and Improve the Quality of Health Services?', Discussion Paper, first meeting of the Working Group on Performance-Based Incentives, Center for Global Development.

Eijkenaar, F., Emmert, M., Scheppan, M. and Schoffski, O. (2013) 'Effects of Pay for Performance in Health Care: A Systematic Review of Systematic Reviews', *Health policy*, Article in press available at: http://dx.doi.org/10.1016/j.healthpol.2013.01.008.

Eising, R. (2004) 'Multilevel Governance and Business Interests in the European Union', *Governance* 17(2): 211–245.

Eldridge, C. and Palmer, N. (2009) 'Performance-Based Payment: Some Reflections on the Discourse, Evidence and Unanswered Questions', *Health Policy and Planning* 24: 160–166.

Emmert, M., Eijkenaar, F., Kemter, H., Esslinger, A.S. and Schoffski, O. (2012) 'Economic Evaluation of Pay-for-Performance in Health Care: A Systematic Review', *European Journal of Health Economics* 13: 755–767.

DOI: 10.1057/9781137500151.0010

Fan, V.Y., Duran, D., Silverman, R. and Glassman, A. (2013) 'Performance-Based Financing at the Global Fund to Fight AIDS, Tuberculosis and Malaria: An Analysis of Grant Ratings and Funding, 2003–12', *Lancet Global Health* 1: e161–e168.

Feachem, R. G. A. and Sabot, O. J. (2006) 'An Examination of the Global Fund at 5 Years', *Lancet* 368: 537–540.

Frenk, J. (2009) 'Strengthening Health Systems to Promote Security', *The Lancet* 373(9682): 2181–2182.

Frenk, J. (2010) 'The Global Health System: Strengthening National Health Systems as the Next Step for Global Progress', *PLoS Medicine* 7(1).

Friedman, J. (2013) 'Do Financial Incentives Undermine the Motivation of Public Sector Workers? Maybe, but Where Is the Evidence from the Field?', *RBF Health Blog* World Bank: Washington http://www.rbfhealth. org/blog/do-financial-incentives-undermine-motivation-public-sector-workers-maybe-where-evidence-field (accessed October 2014).

Fryatt, R., Mills, A. and Nordstrom, A. (2010) 'Financing of Health Systems to Achieve the Health Millennium Development Goals in Low-Income Countries', *Lancet* 375: 419–426.

Global Fund (2001) *The Framework Document of the Global Fund to Fight AIDS, Tuberculosis and Malaria*. Geneva: Global Fund.

Global Fund (2011a) *HIV, Tuberculosis, Malaria and Health and Community Systems Strengthening: Part 5: Health and Community Systems*. 4th Edition., November 2011. Geneva: Global Fund.

Global Fund (2011b) HIV, Tuberculosis, Malaria and Health and Community Systems strengthening: Part 4: Malaria. 4th Edition., November 2011. Geneva: Global Fund.

Harman, S. (2009) 'The World Bank and Global Health', in O. Williams and A. Kay (eds) *The Crisis of Global Health Governance: Challenges, Institutions and Political Economy*. Basingstoke: Palgrave.

Harman S. (2010) *The World Bank and HIV/AIDS: Setting a Global Agenda*. Abingdon: Routledge.

Harmer, A., Spicer, N., Aleshkina, J., Bogdan, D., Chkhatarashvili, K., Muzalieva, G., Rukhadze, N., Samiev, A. and Walt, G. (2012) 'Has Global Fund Support for Civil Society Advocacy in the Former Soviet Union Established Meaningful Engagement or "a Lot of Jabber about Nothing"?', *Health Policy and Planning* 1–10. doi: 10.1093/heapol/czs060.

Hickey, S. and Mohan, G. (2004) 'Towards Participation as Transformation: Critical Themes and Challenges', in S. Hickey and G. Mohan (Eds) *Participation: From Tyranny to Transformation*. London: Zed Books.

DOI: 10.1057/9781137500151.0010

Health Results Innovation Trust Fund (HRITF, 2013) 'Using Results Based Financing to Achieve Maternal and Child Health: Progress Report', *The World Bank*.

HRITF (2014a) RBF Health – Mission. World Bank: Washington. http://www.rbfhealth.org/mission (accessed October 2014).

HRITF (2014b) RBF Health. World Bank: Washington. http://www.rbfhealth.org (accessed October 2014).

Hsu, J., Pitt, C., Greco, G., Berman, P. and Mills, A. (2012) 'Countdown to 2015: Changes in Official Development Assistance to Maternal, Newborn, and Child Health in 2009–10, and Assessment of Progress Since 2003', *Lancet* 380(9848): 1157–1168.

Ifakara Health Institute (2013) Pwani P₄P Evaluation Updates. July, 2013. Advisory Board Meeting, Dar es Salaam, Tanzania.

Ireland, M., Paul, E. and Dujardin, B. (2011) 'Can Performance-Based Financing Be Used to Reform Health Systems in Developing Countries?', *Bulletin of the World Health Organization* 89: 695–698.

Kalk, A. (2011) 'The Costs of Performance-Based Financing', *Bulletin of the World Health Organization* 89: 319.

Kapilashrami, A. and McPake, B. (2013) Transforming Governance or Reinforcing Hierarchies and Competition: Examining the Public and Hidden Transcripts of the Global Fund and HIV in India, *Health Policy and Planning* 28(6): 626–635.

Kelly, K. and Birdsall, K. (2008) *Funding for Civil Society Responses to HIV/AIDS in Tanzania: Status, Problems, Possibilities*. Johannesburg, South Africa: Centre for Aids Development, Research and Evaluation.

Langenbrunner, J. C. and Liu, X. (2005) 'How to Pay? Understanding and Using Payment Incentives', in A. S. Preker and J. C. Langebrunner (eds) *Spending Wisely: Buying Health Services for the Poor*. Washington, DC: World Bank.

Laurell, A. C. and Arellano, O. L. (1996) 'Market Commodities and Poor Relief: The World Bank Proposal for Health', *International Journal of Health Services* 26(1): 1–18.

Lawler, E. E. (1971) *Pay and Organizational Effectiveness: A Psychological View*. New York: McGraw-Hill.

Lawler, E. E. (1989) 'Pay for Performance: Making It Work', *Compensation Benefits Review* 21: 55–60.

Levine, R. and Oomman, N. (2009) 'Global HIV/AIDS Funding and Health Systems: Searching for the Win-Win', *Journal of Acquired Immune Deficiency Syndrome (JAIDS)* 52: S3–S5.

DOI: 10.1057/9781137500151.0010

Leykum, L. K. et al. (2007) 'Organizational Interventions Employing Principles of Complexity Science Have Improved Outcomes for Patients with Type II Diabetes', *Implementation Science* 2(28): 2–28.

Low-Beer, D., Afkhami, H., Komatsu, R., Banati, P., Sempala, M., Katz, I., Cutler, J., Schumacher, P., Tran-Ba-Huy, R. Schwarflander, B. (2007) 'Making Performance-Based Funding Work for Health', *PLoS Medicine* 4(8): e219. doi: 10.1371/journal.pmed.0040219.

Mæstad, O. (2007) 'Rewarding Safe Motherhood: How Can Performance-Based Funding Reduce Maternal and Newborn Mortality in Tanzania', *CMI Report* R2007: 17.

Magrath, P. and Nichter, M. (2012) 'Paying for Performance and the Social Relations of Health Care Provision: An Anthropological Perspective', *Social Science & Medicine* 75: 1778–1785.

Mamdani, M., Mayumana, I., Mashasi, I., Njau, I., Olafsdottir, J., Ipuge, A.E. and Borghie, J. (2012) 'The Role of a "Pay for Performance" (P4P) Scheme in Motivating Health Workers at Different Levels of the Primary Health Care (PHC) System in Tanzania', Poster presented at the Second Global Symposium on Health Systems Research, October 31–November 3, 2012, in Beijing, China. Produced by the Ifakara Health Institute and the London School of Hygiene and Tropical Medicine. Available at: www.ihi.or.tz.

Mamudu, H. M. and Studler, D. T. (2009) 'Multilevel Governance and Shared Sovereignty: EU, Member States and the FCTC', *Governance* 22(1): 73–97.

Marks, G., Hoooghe, L. and Blank, K. (1996) 'European Integration from the 1980s: State-Centric Vs. Multi-Level Governance', *Journal of Common Market Studies* 34(3): 341–378.

Meessen, B. (2013) 'Scaling Up Results-Based Financing for Faster Progress towards the Health MDGs: Reflections on a Recent Donor Meeting in Oslo', *RBF Health Blog* Washington: World Bank. http://www.rbfhealth.org/blog/scaling-results-based-financing-faster-progress-towards-health-mdgs-reflections-recent-donor-o (accessed October 2014).

Meessen, B., Soucat, A. and Sekabaraga, C. (2011) 'Performance-Based Financing: Just a Donor Fad or a Catalyst towards Comprehensive Health-Care Reform?', *Bulletin of the World Health Organization* 89: 153–156.

Ministry of Health (2011) *Operational Implementation Manual for Results-Based Financing (RBF) in Pilot Districts in Zambia*. Lusaka:

DOI: 10.1057/9781137500151.0010

Government of Zambia. http://www.rbfzambia.gov.zm/cside/ contents/docs/Zambia_RBF_Project_Implementation_Manual_ (PIM).pdf (accessed August 2014).

Mlambo, P. (2014) 'Q&A: Pharoah Mlambo Answers 5 Questions About His Work With Rbf Facilities In Gwanda District, Zimbabwe', *RBF Health Blog*. Washington: World Bank. http://www.rbfhealth.org/ blog/qa-pharoah-mlambo-answers-5-questions-about-his-work-rbf-facilities-gwanda-district-zimbabwe (accessed October 2014).

Montagu, D. and Yamey, G. M. (2011) 'Pay-for-Performance and the Millennium Development Goals', *Lancet* 377: 1383–1385.

Oxman, A. D. and Fretheim, A. (2009) 'Can Paying for Results Help to Achieve the Millennium Development Goals? a Critical Review of Selected Evaluations of Results-Based Financing', *Journal of Evidence-Based Medicine* 2: 184–195.

Pitt, C., Greco, G. Powell-Jackson, T. and Mills A. (2010) 'Countdown to 2015: Assessment of Official Development Assistance to Maternal, Newborn, and Child Health, 2003–08', *Lancet* 376(9751): 1485–1496.

Parkinson, J. and Mansbridge, J. (2013) *Deliberative Systems*. Cambridge: Cambridge University Press.

Plsek, P. E. and Wilson, T. (2001) 'Complexity, Leadership, and Management in Healthcare Organisations', *British Medical Journal* 323: 746–749.

Raustiala, K. and Victor, D. G. (2010) 'Regime Complexes in Global Governance', Discussion Paper, Belfer Centre for Science and International Affairs, Harvard University Press: Cambridge.

Ravishankar, N., Gubbins, P., Cooley, R.J., Leach-kemon, K., Michaud, C.M., Jamison, D.T. and Murray, C.J.L. (2009) Financing of Global Health: Tracking Development Assistance for Health from 1990 to 2007, *The Lancet* 373(9681): 2113–2124.

Roenen, C., Ferrinho, P., Van Dormael, M., Conceicao, M.C. and Van Lerberghe, W. (1997) 'How African Doctors Make Ends Meet: An Exploration', *Tropical Medicine & International Health* 2: 127–135.

Schaferhoff, M., Schrade, C. and Schneider, M. (2014) 'The Global Health Financing Architecture and the Millennium Development Goals', in G. W. Brown, G. Yamey and S. Wamala (eds) *Global Health Policy*. London: Willey-Blackwell.

Scheffler, R. M. (2010) 'Pay for Performance (P4P) Programs in Health Services: What Is the Evidence?', *World Health Report*, Background Paper, No. 31.

DOI: 10.1057/9781137500151.0010

Sheikh, K. et al. (2011) 'Building the Field of Health Policy and Systems Research: Framing the Questions', *PLoS Medicine* 8(8).

Shortell, S. M. and Kaluzny, A. (2006) *Health Care Management: Organization Design and Behavior.* 5th Edition. Clifton Park, NY: Thomson Delmar Learning.

Soeters, R., Habineza, C. and Peerenboom, P. B. (2006) 'Performance-Based Financing and Changing the District Health System: Experience from Rwanda', *Bulletin of the World Health Organization* 84: 884–889.

Sridhar, D. and Batniji, R. (2008) 'Misfinancing Global Health: A Case for Transparency in Disbursements and Decision Making', *Lancet* 372: 1185–1191.

Ssengooba, F. McPake, B. and Palmer, N. (2012) 'Why Performance-Based Contracting Failed in Uganda – an "Open-Box" Evaluation of a Complex Health System Intervention', *Social Science and Medicine* 75: 377–383.

Tannis, S. (2014) 'Do Voucher Programs Really Work? 5 Takeaways from a Comprehensive Review of 28 Maternal Health Voucher Schemes', *RBF Health Blog* Washington: World Bank. http://www.rbfhealth.org/blog/do-voucher-programs-really-work-5-takeaways-comprehensive-review-28-maternal-health-voucher (accessed October 2014).

Toonen, J., Canavan, A., Vergeer, P. and Elovainio, R. (2009) *Learning Lessons on Implementing Performance Based Financing, from a Multi-Country Evaluation: A Synthesis Report.* Amsterdam: Royal Tropical Institute.

Town, R., Wholey, D.R., Kralewski, J. and Dowd, B. (2004) 'Assessing the Influence of Incentives on Physicians and Medical Groups', *Medical Care Research and Review* 61(3 Supplement): 80S–118S.

Trisolini, M. G. (2011) 'Theoretical Perspectives on Pay for Performance', in Cromwell et al. (eds) *Pay for Performance in Health Care: Methods and Approaches,* RTI Press publication No. BK-0002-1103. Research Triangle Park, NC: RTI Press.

Vian, T., Miller, C., Themba, Z. and Bukuluki, P. (2012) Perceptions of Per Diems in the Health Sector: Evidence and Implications, *Health Policy and Planning* 2012: 1–10. doi: 10.1093/heapol/czs056.

Witter, S., Fretheim, A., Kessy, F.L. and Lindahl, A.K. (2012) 'Paying for Performance to Improve the Delivery of Health Interventions in Low- and Middle-Income Countries', *Cochrane Database of Systematic Reviews,* Issue 2, Art No.:CD007899. doi: 10.1002/14651858.CD007899.pub2.

DOI: 10.1057/9781137500151.0010

World Bank (2014) Participation and Civic Engagement.
http://web.worldbank.org/WBSITE/EXTERNAL/TOPICS/
EXTSOCIALDEVELOPMENT/EXTPCENG/0,,menuPK:410312~
pagePK:149018~piPK:149093~theSitePK:410306,00.html (accessed
August 2014).
World Health Organisation (2014a) *World Health Statistics 2014.* Geneva:
World Health Organisation. http://apps.who.int/iris/bitstream/10665/
112738/1/9789240692671_eng.pdf?ua=1 (accessed August 2014).
World Health Organisation (2014b) *Twelfth sProgramme of Work – Not
merely the absence of disease.* Geneva: World Health Organisation.
http://apps.who.int/iris/bitstream/10665/112792/1/GPW_2014-
2019_eng.pdf?ua=1 (accessed August 2014).

Anonymised Interviews

GEN1 Global Fund to Fight AIDS, Tuberculosis and Malaria, September
2013.
GEN2 World Health Organisation, September 2013.
GEN3 World Health Organisation, September 2013.
GEN4 Global Fund to Fight AIDS, Tuberculosis and Malaria,
September 2013.
GEN5 UNAIDS, September 2013.
GEN6 World Health Organisation, September 2013.
GEN 7 World Health Organisation, September 2013.
SA1 NGO, February 2013.
SA2 SANAC, February 2013.
SA3 UNAIDS, February 2013.
SA4 SANAC, March 2013.
SA5 Department of Health, February 2013.
SA6 UNFPA, February 2013.
SA7 Medical Research Council, February 2013.
SA8 Western Cape District Health Services, February 2013.
SA9 SANAC, February 2013.
SA10 Foundation, February 2013.
SA11 Desmond Tutu TB Centre Tygerberg Hospital, Western Cape,
February 2013.
SA12 Ministry of Health, March 2013.
TNZ1 NGO, October 2012.

DOI: 10.1057/9781137500151.0010

TNZ2 NGO, October 2012.

TNZ3 Research Institute, November 2013.

TNZ4 GIZ, October 2012.

TNZ5 DANIDA, October 2012.

TNZ6 WHO, October 2012.

TNZ7 Ministry of Health and Social Welfare, October 2012.

TNZ8 PWC, October 2012.

TNZ9 CHAI, October 2012.

WAS1 USAID, September 2012.

WAS2 World Bank, September 2012.

WAS3 World Bank, September 2012.

WAS4 World Bank, September 2012.

ZAM1 Ministry of Community Development and Mother and Child Health, June 2013.

ZAM2 NGO, November 2012.

ZAM3 Ministry of Health and Social Welfare, November 2012.

ZAM4 District Medical Office, Katete, October 2013.

ZAM5 District Health Centre, Katete, October 2013.

DOI: 10.1057/9781137500151.0010

Index

DOI: 10.1057/9781137500151.0011

DOI: 10.1057/9781137500151.0011